DANTE'S ROAD

The Journey Home for the Modern Soul

DANTE'S ROAD

The Journey Home for the Modern Soul

MARC THOMAS SHAW

Anamchara Books
Vestal, New York 13850
www.AnamcharaBooks.com

paperback ISBN: 978-1-62524-493-2
ebook ISBN: 978-1-62524-494-9

Drawings and interior design by Micaela Grace.
Cover design by Publishing Soul.
www.PublishingSoul.com

to Soren

Contents

Acknowledgements

Thank you to the many authors who influenced this book—in particular, Professor Thorpe, who himself has two excellent books in print: *Rapture of the Deep* and *Wisdom Sings the World*. The central books of his class must also be included here, given their deep and abiding influence: Homer's *Odyssey*, Dante's *The Divine Comedy*, Dostoevsky's *The Brothers Karamazov*, and Czeslaw Milosz's poetry anthology *Book of Luminous Things*. In addition, Julia Cameron's *The Artist's Way* has been deeply influential, both personally and in providing some of the structure of the present work.

The writings of Anthony De Mello, Father Thomas Keating, and Father Richard Rohr have been influential throughout, both in introducing and affirming many of the ideas present. Also connected with these ideas is of course Joseph Campbell's *Hero with a Thousand Faces*, as well as the work of Northrop Frye, James Frazer, Carl Jung, and beyond that, the myths themselves.

I must also acknowledge my many students over the years who helped hone my framing of questions and exercises, as well as the many friends and family members who walked through chapters or exercises and provided invaluable feedback. To my wife Karla, who provided valuable feedback at every step, and my son, Soren, who provided the motivation. Thank you!

A Personal Preface

In early 2014 I found myself half asleep in a college campus auditorium, surrounded by a couple thousand cheering audience members, while I tried to figure out what I was doing there. My two-year-old son had a cold and a fever, which meant I hadn't gotten much sleep for several days, and I was struggling to stay awake. But there I was at what I had expected to be a writer's conference.

Instead, this Storyline Conference, held once a year and sponsored by author Donald Miller, was intended to inspire people to live better stories, with resources to help writers, bloggers, and marketers get going with their work. Writers came and went from the stage to tell their stories, interviewed by Miller himself. Depending on who came on stage, a different little section of the audience burst out in wild cheers.

I wasn't a rabid fan of any of them, and I was only at the conference because someone had given my wife and me tickets to it—but I was looking for some kind of inspiration. I'd been stuck about halfway through a novel for years. The book was a train wreck. And worse: writing it wasn't any fun. Now, as I sat with my thoughts, gulping coffee, I realized something.

I had been putting pressure on myself to write a great novel *seen through the eyes of someone else*. I wanted pretty much everyone in the entire world to like it, but when it came right down to it, I didn't particularly want to write the novel; what I actually wanted was mainstream literary appreciation. But now I was listening to writer after writer who had simply written from the gut about their own experience. Even if what they wrote wasn't for everyone, it resonated with someone!

I began to wonder: What would happen if I were to write from my gut? What would be fun to write? What would be fun to read? What did I enjoy reading the most? And why?

The book that came to my mind was Julia Cameron's *Artist's Way*. This book doesn't point out the flaws with society or religion or the way we're living. Instead, it's helpful. It's constructive. It's life-giving. And I realized—*that's* the kind of thing I wanted to write. Something that would help others grow, to experience transformation, to move toward wholeness.

My thoughts then turned to what had inspired me most in my life—the great myths, the great poets, the great works from across the wisdom traditions, the teachings and practices of the mystics and contemplatives. These all taught that profound healing and genuine transformation is possible. A life of vitality and fullness is actually available, and these stories, poems, and teachings had helped me confront my own shadow. Because of them, I had experienced healing and come out on the other side. Slowly but surely, I'd experienced for myself the change described by the mystics and ancient storytellers.

Meanwhile, I saw those close to me struggling through life, stuck in arrested development, in addiction, ineffectiveness, immature patterns, failed marriages, lifeless careers, loneliness, and depression. Their lives so often lacked the vitality and fullness described by the great poets, mystics, and spiritual teachers. Whether my friends and acquaintances called themselves Christian or not didn't seem to matter much, because the pattern in their lives was largely the same—short periods of satisfaction or achievement that gave way to long stretches of struggle and suffering.

I wanted to share my own journey with them, not because I thought I was better than they were, but because I knew this path was what they also needed. But how, I wondered, could I communicate something like this in an accessible way? The writings of the poets, mystics, and contemplatives aren't exactly light reading and certainly not everyone's cup of tea, even for avid readers. I had needed years of study and practice to get a handle on the message these writings carry.

My passion for poetry and myth seemed far away from people caught in their everyday struggles. As I searched for a bridge to span this distance, I remembered a line one of my mentors, a college English professor, said when explaining a work of literature: *We're lost. We're trying to get home.* I realized now—*that's* what we all have in common. It's as true today for ordinary people living ordinary lives as it was for the world's great mythmakers and storytellers. And one way to read the myths is as a road map of the soul's journey to God. The soul's journey *home*.

Instantly, I thought of Dante and his pilgrimage down through Hell, up Mount Purgatory, and into Paradise. In *The Divine Comedy*, Dante gives us a model of the soul's journey home. He lays out the path of the spiritual life—first down into the depths, then the climb upward, and finally the moment of vision when the spiritual world becomes real and present.

That moment, sitting in a conference I never would have attended if not for the chance gift of the tickets, was the seed of inspiration that grew into this book. Dante's *Divine Comedy* became the foundation for the three sections of this book: the Downward Way, the Outward Way, and the Upward Gaze.

As I worked on the book, I rediscovered the writings of the ancient Christian mystics, as well as modern teachers like Richard Rohr, Cynthia Bourgeault, and Father Thomas Keating, who reinterpret these ancient teachings for a modern audience using the language of both Christian tradition and modern psychology. Fresh connections became evident to me, and from them I constructed a new framework. I had found a modern roadmap of the sacred journey to personal breakthrough and a life of vitality and meaning, a map that draws on ancient myth and spirituality, personal experience, and contemporary psychology.

The writing went quickly. It was as if I were being given each section from an external source as the pieces clicked into place. As I began the final sections of the book I had a further transformational experience that confirmed my work even more deeply.

In my personal contemplative practice and reading, I circled back through old wounds of my own, and there I found deep reservoirs of inner guilt, shame, and failure that I had failed to drain in my previous soul work. In a profound experience of inner release, I had an awakening into deep Oneness that lasted for about a week. It was a kind of inner transfiguration in which all concern and anxiety, all self-consciousness, were absolutely gone. While I dwelled in that space, I knew there was nothing to fear. Nothing to achieve. Only deep acceptance. The fruits of this experience were an abiding joy and a much deeper capacity for genuine selfless love. I felt a surge of energy and an influx of grace that sustained me for months afterward.

This state of complete at-one-ment, of being-at-home with the indwelling Spirit, is what the great mystics experienced. This is also how Jesus lived during his time on earth; it's what he called the Kingdom. But Jesus, like the mystics, had no illusions about how to reach this holy place in all its fullness. He knew he would have to face the ultimate sacrifice of his physical self, to descend into the valley, experience the wounds, and face the shadow—and then to own it and move through it. I believe this is what Jesus meant in the Gospel when he asked us to take up our cross and follow him on a way of radical transformation and inner resurrection. When we "die"—emotionally, spiritually, intellectually—all that was dead within us will come to life once more.

As I pondered these ideas, reading and rereading the poets and mystics both ancient and modern, I realized this book is trans-religious. The message it carries is not only for Christians, though that is my personal background and my own experience is largely from Christian wisdom traditions. Instead, it is for anyone looking to access the deeper spiritual truths that are encoded in our very souls. These truths penetrate more deeply than any religious doctrine or tribal affiliation. The pathway of freedom, wholeness, and healing is not particular to any one tradition, but universally available.

Guided by the wisdom of Dante and other ancient teachers, I invite you to take this journey. The road ahead will lead through your inner depths and wounds, to the sacrifice of the ego, and then on to fulfillment, the sacred space where you will find sacramental ways of living. It's not an easy journey. It takes courage to do soul work, to look into the abyss—the areas of your inner being you're afraid to face. I hope I can help you find the track that leads through this experience, but only you can answer the questions you'll face along the way:

What is my Hell—and how do I move through it?

What is my Purgatory—and what lessons do I need to learn there?

What is my Paradise—and how do I get there?

The process of writing and bringing this book to publication has been like watching a flower come into bloom. If it never found a single reader, this unfurling would still have been life-giving—but the wisdom I have learned is not meant to be hoarded. Spiritual lessons, like love, are enriched in the giving, and I was granted the gift of walking the journey and mapping it so that I could in turn offer it to you.

May the Divine One who is ever present within you reveal new insights in the very depths of your own being as you journey through this book.

Peace and blessings,

Marc Thomas Shaw
San Diego, May 2018

If we don't learn to mythologize our lives, inevitably we will pathologize them.

-RICHARD ROHR

We're Lost

And We're Trying to Get Home

At the beginning of Dante's epic poem, the pilgrim wakes up lost in a dark wood, filled with a sense of dread, alone and uncertain as to how he got there. He makes his way to the edge of the dense forest, where the early morning light gives him a ray of hope that he might escape. Immediately, however, his upward way is blocked by three ferocious beasts: a spotted leopard, a ravenous lion, and a she-wolf. Despairing, he shrinks back down into the dark wood. He's still lost.

This is how the story opens. Like so many great works of myth and literature, in the beginning, the hero is lost—and that is the central insight of the great writers and poets into the human condition as a whole:

We're lost. We're trying to get home.

This is where so many of us find ourselves. We hit particular points in our lives and realize we're disoriented, looking for a way out, for a sense of wholeness or fulfillment, only to find our way blocked by life circumstance, by addictive patterns, by fear.

We're lost. We're trying to get home.

Whether it's Homer's Odysseus stranded on an island, a struggling addict, or a young mother making her way through a bitter divorce, this sense of profound disorientation is a universal experience. How do we find our way? Where does healing come from? One powerful way to read ancient myths and the work of great poets is as a map of the soul's journey home. They teach us how to navigate our lives toward a sense of meaning, communion, and wholeness.

THE DIVINE COMEDY

Dante Alighieri's fourteenth-century masterpiece *The Divine Comedy* maps out this territory through metaphor and allegory. In this epic poem, written while he was in exile, Dante gives a picture of his own spiritual journey. Drawing on his immense learning, he touches on big issues like history and empire, justice and morality, education and learning, cosmology and theology, and the role of art in our lives, all filtered through a medieval Christian imagination. Most important for our purposes, though, the poem is an account of the soul's journey toward God, the soul's journey *home*.

Dante—who is also the protagonist of the story—wakes up in the dark wood three days before Easter Sunday in the year 1300. After being confronted by the three beasts, which represent the human vices of lust, pride, and greed, Dante falls into despair. But then something unexpected happens. He experiences a grace. A guide comes to him in the form of the classical poet Virgil, the poet of discipline and virtue.

Virgil guides Dante down through nine circles of Hell, where he learns the fate of those who have died in their various sins and vices, the lustful, the wrathful, the gluttonous, and so on. The people he meets along his way include historical, biblical, and mythical figures, from Hercules and Medusa to Pope Boniface VIII. Finally, Dante sees Lucifer himself, trapped in ice at the bottom of Hell, beating his wings and gnawing forever at the three traitors of church and empire—Brutus, Cassius, and Judas Iscariot.

Having learned the lessons from his guide about the moral order at work in creation, Dante can finally leave this mythical Hell. He climbs down the side of Lucifer's body, turns upside down, and comes out into the clear air. In front of him he sees the steep slope of Mount Purgatory.

On this seven-story mountain, people go through a process of purification with tasks assigned to them to correct their distorted loves and selfishness. Here, too, Dante has lessons to learn. As he begins his climb up the mountain, an angel etches seven P's into his forehead, which stand for *peccatum*, a sin or wound. At each stage of the climb, the brush of an angel's wing wipes one of the P's off the pilgrim's forehead until he is made fully clean. Finally, at the top of the mountain, Dante passes through a wall of fire and steps into the garden of Eden. His guide Virgil, who represents virtue and reason, can take him no farther.

Dante's childhood love, the beautiful and virtuous Beatrice, becomes his new guide, leading him on a journey up through the ten spheres of Paradise. The highest spheres in Paradise are populated by contemplatives and mystics, who open themselves to the direct encounter with God. Finally, at the end of his journey, Dante arrives at a rose of flame with Christ at the center, the faithful dispersed on the petals of the rose, angels like bees flying from soul to soul to minister.

Based on a medieval imagination of the afterlife, the poem can be graphic in its depiction of suffering, but it also gives a moving portrait of the soul's journey toward God, the soul's journey home. Most useful for us, the poem provides a framework for thinking about our spiritual lives.

The spiritual path requires us to wake up, to move down through our personal hell of confusion, disorientation, and suffering, to see our own wounds. As many of the mystics recognize, we rise only through falling. To come to the land of love, we have to pass through the pains of death. We have to do the work of deep recognition. We have to confront the reality of our suffering, trace the roots of our harmful patterns, which usually grow out from our woundedness. We need to see our reality as it is and accept it. This brings about a process of maturation. Understanding our *particular* ego patterns allows us to live in freedom and to cultivate compassion more deeply for others. It enables us to be more present and aware in the world moment to moment. It empowers us to go about the work of service in the world. Understanding also gives us a sober assessment of our strengths and weaknesses. It recognizes areas for growth and guides us toward a clear sense of purpose.

This stage of maturation, which involves identifying our work in the world, is like climbing Mount Purgatory, as we become more and more refined in our goals, our self-understanding, and capacity to give. Even with the best of intentions, though, we find vestiges of the ego keeping us from our full flowering.

This calls for the next stage of the spiritual journey, which is like Dante's journey through the realm of Paradise. Even if we already recognize we are held in a perfect love, we continually submit ourselves to the refining process of that love. As we engage in learning, healthy community, and some form of contemplative practice, we allow Divine therapy to take place. We learn to identify more and more with Divine love, and allow our False Self or ego to dissolve more and more. We cultivate a disposition of openness, acceptance, presence, and love. This is the ongoing process of inner refinement. This is the sacred journey.

But before we can start the journey we have to recognize the truth of our situation, whether we're bored or anxious or addicted or depressed.

We're lost. We're trying to get home.

This is where we begin.

THEOLOGICAL AND HISTORICAL FOUNDATION

The spiritual journey outlined in this book harkens back to both the old myths, the ancient practice of pilgrimage, and Christian mystical theology. Whether traveling the Camino de Santiago or traveling to Graceland, people are looking for an experience of the transcendent. The outward journey is a means of inner transformation. This is a journey we take when we feel stuck, fragmented, out of touch with ourselves and with the Divine. It situates us within a larger story. It gives us insight into the nature of reality and our role in the world. There are many tributaries from the Christian tradition running into this river.

One of these tributaries is the story of Abraham, called forth by YHWH from the city of Ur to journey home to "the land that I shall show you."[1] Another is the story of Moses, wandering through the desert following the path toward the Promised Land. The Hebrew scriptures identify three festivals, Passover, the Festival of Weeks, and the Festival of Booths, during which the people were collectively to return to God.[2] These were pilgrimage festivals during which time the people were to return to Jerusalem to offer tithes and sacrifices, to reaffirm their identity as a people under God's covenant. In each of these cases, pilgrimage involved expanded awareness, restoration, or a return to wholeness through ritual participation in the collective myth; it reaffirmed a deeper identity beyond everyday social roles. Christ himself entered the wilderness to undergo his final preparations for ministry in the Gospel account. He left the everyday norms behind and entered the liminal space of transformation.[3]

Many biblical stories have a recurring motif of revelations on the road. God revealed himself to Jacob on the road at Bethel.[4] Christ revealed himself to disciples on the road to Emmaus[5] and to Paul on the road to Damascus.[6] From the lives of the saints to *The Divine Comedy* to *Pilgrim's Progress*, the idea of pilgrimage and the image of the journey as a metaphor for the spiritual life has had a lasting hold on the imagination.

We're trying to get home.

Yet another tributary flowing into this book and the treatment of contemplative practices as central to this journey is the tradition of mystical or *apophatic theology*. Christian tradition distinguishes between two main strands of theology: *kataphatic*, or affirming, and *apophatic*, or negative, theology. Kataphatic theology is based on concepts and images for God. It's been the dominant form of theological expression and teaching since the Enlightenment. We see it today in sermons and worship songs, as well as in theology classrooms and Bible studies and books. This theology is positive and constructive. It affirms the attributes of God and forms a conceptual basis for the spiritual life. At the same time, it organizes our understanding and situates us in relationship to God and community. It's a story we tell ourselves about who God is.

For contemplatives, though, this is only part of the picture. The spiritual life has a further dimension once we understand that our concepts, conditioning, and culture are inherently limited. We come to understand God is more than we can conceive of intellectually or put into words. Ultimately, God is Mystery, to be experienced more than to be understood. This is the beginning of negative theology, a teaching that stretches back at least to early church fathers like Clement of Alexandria, Gregory of Nyssa, and Dionysius the Areopagite, and flows through many mystics and contemplatives over the centuries. As we enter into this experience, we come to see that our understanding and therefore our practices and spiritual growth are limited by our cultural context and our unconscious assumptions. Like Dante trying to climb out of the forest, we confront our own limitations through the apophatic viewpoint.

We are not trapped. Grace extends far beyond our limitations. From a contemplative perspective, it's when we reach the end of ourselves that we are open to encounter the God who transcends the mental image we've built. Rather, we encounter the One Who Is, what the Hebrew scriptures call the I AM. We do this by entering into silence. In doing so, we go for a little while beyond the mind and let go of the concepts we cling to, allowing even our subconscious to be subjected to God's transforming presence. This is where transformation takes place.

For many of us, this search usually occurs in response to a crisis of faith or a deep encounter with suffering. Some part of us is deeply threatened. The old categories, the simplistic ways of thinking about life, identity, our journey, or even our ideas about God no longer hold, and we move into deeper waters. When we are here, out of our depth, a new stage of maturity in the spiritual life begins. John of the Cross called this *the Night of Sense*, when the usual consolations we cling to dry up. When we move past our certainties and concepts, we move into the contemplative space.

For the Eastern monks, a common form of contemplative prayer was called *hesychasm*, which translates as stillness, rest, or silence. Based on Christ's invitation in

Matthew 6:6 to "enter the inner room, close the door and pray to the Father in secret," the hesychast rests silently for a direct experience of God. This tradition of resting silently in the presence of God is carried on today in practices like contemplative prayer or Lectio Divina, which we will touch on in more depth later in the book. As we grow into deeper experience of these kinds of practices, we move into greater intimacy with God, more and more open to the transforming Presence.[7]

The first step as we begin this journey is to encounter the reality of suffering, to realize the stakes of the game, of what can happen when we don't go through this process of transformation: *we pass on our pain.* It will spread out from us to others, both those who are close to us, as well as those of whom we are less aware yet whose lives we still influence. It will be our invisible inheritance to the next generation, a heavy burden they will continue to shoulder even when we are gone.

But we have another option. Just as Dante walks downward through the nine circles of Hell, grappling with the various torments he encounters, we will walk our own journeys of the Downward Way, entering into the darkness of our own caves, exploring both the conscious and unconscious suffering we experience in the world, in our families, and in our own lives. Equipped with this deeper self-knowledge, we then move along the Outward Way, or into the world, experiencing a newfound sense of direction and orientation, just as Dante uses his climb up Mount Purgatory as an occasion to reflect on vocation and purpose. With a deeper understanding and a clear-eyed but gracious gaze toward our own faults, we have the freedom to change our relationship to the world around us, establishing healthy rhythms of rest, of play, of work, and a greater awareness for others and how we might serve them, given our unique experiences and temperament.

Finally, just as Dante learns from the divine Beatrice and the mystic Bernard of Clairvaux as he moves toward his final vision of God, we turn our gaze upward, opening ourselves to the refining process of letting go, of deepening love, and of the transforming mystery as taught by the great mystics and contemplatives through the ages.

But to begin our journey takes a sober assessment of where so many of us are in the here and now. *We're lost. We're trying to get home.*

With the reflections and exercises in this book, I'm inviting you to enter the gateway into this journey. I want to offer you some guidance along the path, to help you get oriented and start out in the right direction. In this book, you'll find spiritual food and guidance from some of the great teachers of the perennial and Christian traditions. I'm inviting you to take Dante's road along with me, following in the footsteps he left behind in his account of the soul's journey.

DESIGN
The Reading

This book is designed with the working adult in mind. Starting with the reality that most of us today have busy lives, this book is intended to be read one chapter a time. Each reading includes imaginative or participative sections to help visualize and experience the process of transformation by following the wayposts of the mythical journey. When you come to these sections, it may help to stop, take a breath, and even close your eyes once you've read through the description to imagine yourself in that space and to experience it in as much detail as possible.

As you go through the reading, go ahead and underline, circle, copy down, whatever. Consume however you consume, but the material works best if you maintain this simple waypost-by-waypost rhythm. It may be helpful to schedule a reading time, commit to it, and write it down, the way you would any other important activity in your life. Think of one thirty-minute stretch of free time you have to complete the reading in the week ahead and enter that below. Then, picture where you will most likely be during that time and write that in, too.

> **I WILL READ AT:**
>
> Day: _____
>
> Start time: _____ End time: _____
>
> I will be in: _____

Exercises

Congratulations, you've just finished your first spiritual exercise! That is, setting aside a time for reflection and spiritual exercise. Sounds too simple to be worthwhile? Far from it. Subtle but intentional shifts can have long-lasting and far-reaching impact on our overall well-being and sense of purpose.

At the end of each reading, there will be a list of optional exercises to choose from. I recommend picking at least two or three, but pick what resonates with you at the time. Different people learn differently, and I have included different types of reflection and learning experiences to go with each reading, including writing, experiential learning, music, art, and poetry suggestions. The songs listed here are from my own mental playlist, but I have also provided a personal playlist worksheet at the back, in case you would like to insert your own track listing to pair with each waypost's main theme. Since this book is intended to be used not just once but perhaps several times, whenever the reader feels stuck over the course of life, it might be helpful to use the provided songs the first time through, and then choose your own songs once you have a feel for the process. Alternatively, you can turn to the back of the book and fill in the songs that fit best for you with each topic. Make it work for you.

Small-Group Discussion

One of the most powerful ways we experience change is in community. Talking through our experiences and reflecting out loud to others consolidates new insights and solidifies change in our identities. Through this process, we are reflecting on our own personal stories and giving them new shape and meaning. Because of this, I recommend this book as a useful tool for groups. Our stories are meant to be told!

Groups built around this book should be intimate spaces, with around three to five members, although it can be more, if the members already have a high comfort level with each other. Why so few? Because a small space is an intimate space, and what we don't want is contrived conversation. In American culture, especially among males, spaces for emotional honesty and vulnerability are very hard to come by. A small-group setting with a few trusted intimates works best. Use your intuition here. If you don't have access to close confidants in your geographical area, think of a few people that you don't know well yet but with whom you feel comfortable or have a sense of possible connection. Another option in our world of global connectedness is to get together with people over the Internet. This could even be a means of staying more closely connected with people with whom you may have fallen out of touch.

Even if you don't have the time or means to connect with a small group, I strongly recommend finding one close friend or partner with whom you can verbally process your movement and experience. This allows you to get feedback on some of your core issues from someone else's perspective as you move through this landscape. In the Greek myth of Theseus and the Minotaur, it is Ariadne who holds the guiding thread as the hero Theseus moves through the labyrinth to confront the monster. Consider who your Ariadne will be before you begin.

SMALL GROUP BRAINSTORM

List up to six people you would consider starting a group with:

1. _____

2. _____

3. _____

4. _____

5. _____

6. _____

When and where might you be able to meet on a regular basis?

Time: _____

Place: _____

With an understanding of who your travel partners will be, or whether yours will be a solitary journey, you can open the gate that leads to your journey. All you need is a sense of adventure and an openness to being transformed along the way. But first, to know where we're going, we'll need to get oriented.

NOTES

1. Genesis 12:1

2. Deuteronomy 16:16

3. For a deeper treatment of transformation and liminal or "threshold" spaces, see Victor Turner's *The Ritual Process*.

4. Genesis 28:10–19

5. Luke 24:13–32

6. Acts 9:39

7. Thomas Keating. *Invitation to Love: The Way of Christian Contemplation* (Rockport, MA: Element, 1992).

The journey home begins when the soul leaves its state of union with God. Born into this world, we learn to look for our true being and find the way back to our Beloved.

–LLEWELLYN VAUGHAN-LEE

It is the business of each of us to try to arrive at wholeness and harmony: of mind within itself, of heart with mind, of action with heart—and the beginning of this journey is to see, and suffer, the fact that we are not now whole; that we are, as was Dante at the beginning of his journey, "lost in a Dark Wood."

–MARTHA HEYNEMAN

Waking Up

The Gateway to
the Inner Journey

We begin with a new awareness of the reality of our life. In Dante's words, at the opening of his story:

> In the middle of the journey of my life, I came to myself in a dark wood, where the direct way was lost. It is a hard thing to speak of, how wild, harsh and impenetrable that wood was, so that thinking of it recreates the fear. It is scarcely less bitter than death: but in order to tell of the good that I found there, I must tell of the other things I saw there.

I cannot rightly say how I entered it. I was so full of sleep, at that point where I abandoned the true way.

Most of us have had this experience. Somewhere along the way, without even recognizing what we were doing, we went astray. We got off the path we were meant to follow. We find ourself in a place we don't want to be.

This entryway into the spiritual journey is about confronting some of the painful realities in the world and ourselves. Much of our lives are organized around protecting ourselves against such pain. In fact, neuro-chemically, this is exactly what our addictions provide: a temporary, manufactured means of pain management. And we all have our favorite protections, ranging from something as simple as a nostalgic clinging to the past to endless television consumption to drugs and sexual addictions.

When we pay any attention to these shadow aspects of ourselves—whatever our particular external hang-up may be—we tend to feel shame. Or we may do our best to resist that shame by railing against an oppressive society, insisting on our freedom to be who we are. But ultimately, none of this lets us live with freedom and vitality.

This process has become so deeply entrenched in our society that pain management is a huge source of profit. In the last twenty years alone, drug prescription has skyrocketed, with pharmaceuticals raking in higher profits than any other industry. Our society seems to create the brokenness, and then offer a solution to it for a price. As Wendell Berry writes,

> The modern urban-industrialized society is based on a series of radical disconnections between body and soul, husband and wife, marriage and community, community and the earth. At each of these points of disconnection the collaboration of corporation, government, and expert sets up a profit-making enterprise that results in the further dismemberment and impoverishment of the Creation.[1]

The great spiritual traditions teach that only in *facing* pain, through entering into our suffering, do we grow into spiritual maturity. When we turn and confront our suffering, it can become a means of transformation toward humility, compassion, and selfless love. In the Christian tradition, this is the Paschal Mystery (from the Greek word for suffering, *pascho*), the refining transformation of pain. Uncovering our areas of suffering, especially in the context of community, provides both a point of connection with others as well as a means of deeper awareness of ourselves.

From a Jungian perspective, this is the process of facing, owning, and integrating the shadow, which allows us to become what Henri Nouwen calls a Wounded Healer, someone who has examined the heart's wounds, acknowledged them, and is then able to lead others from this position of vulnerability. This is how long-term, authentic community is built. We are invited to walk that same path of Christ's Passion,[2] facing the reality of cruelty inflicted upon the world and the wounds inflicted upon ourselves. Without identifying our own wound, articulating it, and moving toward wholeness, we become trapped by it. It defines us.

We are lost.

As author and Franciscan monk Richard Rohr puts it, "If we do not transform our pain, we will most assuredly transmit it."[3] Toxic examples of people living primarily out of their wounds are all around us. Billions of people living out of their wounds pour out the dangerous cocktail of our current world.

Part of moving toward spiritual maturity means making a conscious decision to grow. One way to do this is by undertaking what I'm calling "the mythical journey." It's the path through the wound to a new sense of identity and wholeness. The first steps necessarily take us downward and inward toward our core wound. It can be dark there.

But first, we have to recognize we're lost. We have to understand our situation. We have to *wake up*. Once we do, we can begin our journey.

NOTES

1. Berry, Wendell. *The Unsettling of America: Culture & Agriculture* (San Francisco, CA: Sierra Club Books, 1977), page 136.

2. The word "passion," when referring to Christ's experience on the cross, has to do with older meanings of the word. The Latin roots of the word imply meanings such as enduring, undergoing an experience, and suffering, much like the experience of a woman in labor.

3. Richard Rohr. *Things Hidden: Scripture as Spirituality* (London: SPCK Publishing, 2016), page 25.

We have not even to risk the adventure alone for the heroes of all time have gone before us; the labyrinth is thoroughly known; we have only to follow the thread of the hero-path. And where we had thought to find an abomination, we shall find a God; where we had thought to slay another, we shall slay ourselves; where we had thought to travel outward, we shall come to the center of our own existence; where we had thought to be alone, we shall be with all the world.

–JOSEPH CAMPBELL

PART ONE

The Downward Way

The paschal mystery—the way of suffering—means God is somehow participating in the suffering of humans and creation, instead of just passively tolerating it and observing it, that changes everything—at least for those who are willing to "gaze" contemplatively. All humble, suffering souls can learn this from the flow of life itself. It all depends on whether you have "gazed" long and deep enough at the paradoxical mystery of life and death.

-RICHARD ROHR

Into the Cave

Waypost One

After realizing he needs to get back on course, Dante tries to go upward—but he finds his path forward blocked by three terrifying beasts. As he slips back down into the dark of the forest, he's startled by an approaching figure he can only dimly make out. It turns out to be the classical poet Virgil, who will be Dante's guide through the first two stages of his journey.

Virgil tells Dante he will never defeat the beasts with his own power. Going that way, he'll only be torn apart. To taste true freedom, he'll have to take a different path—the downward path into darkness. He'll have to go underground.

When Dante's hears about the road ahead, walking the downward way where he will be forced to confront the reality of suffering, he turns pale with fear. He has to steel himself for the journey ahead, what he calls *the inner war.* He's not sure his mind, his intellect, his will, and his heart are prepared.

But Virgil reassures him that this journey, though difficult, is ultimately a gift, a grace. Messengers from the heavenly realms have sent Virgil to guide Dante along this road of insight, revelation, and self-understanding. The gateway to the underworld bears the inscription, "Abandon all hope, ye who enter here"—but emboldened by Virgil's words, Dante is now willing to walk through the mouth of the cave and step into the enveloping dark.

You, too, have a journey to make as you read this book. To follow Dante's road, you'll need your imagination; otherwise, you may be intellectually interested in what I have to say, but you'll fail to interact with it deeply and intimately. Some of us are already aware of our fears, our hang-ups, and our mental addictions, but others need more prompting to do the inner exploration this path requires—and that can be uncomfortable.

Moving from paragraphs that are more idea-based and less personal into sections that require your imaginative participation may be difficult, so my advice is to pause and take a breath whenever you see the word IMAGINE. View that word as an invitation to open your mind and shift your consciousness a bit before you read on. And so . . .

IMAGINE

As your journey begins, you open your eyes to find yourself in a forest with thick foliage swaying overhead. A growing light filters down through the leaves, and for a moment, you have the sense of a memory just out of reach, the whisper of a fading song on the breeze. You yawn, blink, and test the air with your nose. Ahead, you see a place where the light is shining more brightly, indicating a break in the trees, and you head in that direction. A small path leads you around a sheer rock face and opens into a small clearing at the mouth of a cave. You look in all directions, uncertain where to go next, but the only path you see is the one that leads into the cave.

As you step closer to the cave, you notice that the air feels damper against your skin. Feel the forest floor beneath your feet, and hear the crunch of dried leaves, twigs, and pine needles underfoot. See the moss and lichen on the jagged rock around the cave. The light grows brighter in the distance beyond the mountain, and you realize the sun has only just risen. You're tired, and you'd like to go back to sleep—but the knowledge settles over you that there's no other way out of your current situation except the pathway that leads into the cave.

This is mythical space, inner space, resonant and alive. What dangers wait for you in the cave? What inner change do you fear most? As you move inside, you leave behind the light of day, all that was clearly visible to you in the external world. In the shadows, you become disoriented.

The downward journey, this descent into the underworld, is a consistent pattern in the world's myths. The great heroes have to pass through the darkness to learn their greater purpose, to learn the way home. According to the Christian story, we are born into exile, displaced wanderers who yearn to find our way back to Paradise. Once we wake up to our situation, the first step on the journey home is downward, into the cave.

The mouth of the cave, for our purposes, is the recognition that something has to change. Our default identity, our False Self, wants its cravings and desires fulfilled. This is its way of controlling life and warding off fear. For addicts, the first step toward recovery is acknowledging that their lives have become unmanageable—and we all have our forms of addiction. We all rely on things to manage our pain and anxiety, even if they're only habitual thought patterns. Eventually, something forces us to see that the thing on which we've relied isn't taking care of the problem. In fact, it's making it worse. We enter the cave out of the recognition that something has to change; our normal walls of self-protection may have once seemed effective, but now they've become a prison.

The wisdom traditions teach that before new life can begin, a death is always required. We can't escape the prison of addiction and selfishness until we die to our habitual ways of being. We must die to our normal understanding of who we are for change to occur, for healing to begin, for love to become possible. This waypost is about intentionally engaging in that process of going inward, of dying to our normal patterns of ego protection.

There can be many entry points into this first stage of the journey, when we recognize something has to change. It might be the death of a loved one that causes us to question our faith or our fundamental worldview. It can be the loss of a job we deeply identified with—or the loss of a dream that gave us a sense of meaning and purpose. It might be that a relationship, one we thought was the bedrock of our lives, suddenly breaks into pieces. Whatever it is, some kind of destabilizing force usually nudges us (or shoves us) into the process of transformation.

My first experience of this happened toward the end of my time in seminary, when I experienced a combination of deaths that led to deep disorientation. My parents, who had spent the past sixteen years working in church-based missions in Europe, were coming back to America—which meant that the place I thought of as *home* would no longer be available to me. I had come to rely on twice-yearly trips to recharge while I reconnected with old friends, family, and familiar places, finding once again a sense of intimate community and identity—but now I would not have access anymore to that place of safety and nurturing. At the same time, my master's degree program was ending. I was at a loss as to my next steps in life. Should I continue my schooling—or start paying off loans? If so, what kind of job should I look for? In what town? I asked for advice from friends and family, but there were no easy answers. At the same time, my dad was struggling with health issues, and my mom reached out frequently to give updates and prayer requests; they too were in uncertain terrain now. I felt deeply disoriented.

In the midst of that upheaval, while I was getting together with several high school friends, another friend of ours called on the phone, sobbing, hardly intelligible. "He just shot them," she choked out. "He just up and shot them." When she calmed down a little, she said that three of our other friends from high school had been shot in a home invasion, two of them fatally.

Stunned, we tried to make calls to find out what had happened. When that failed, we raced through the vendors and street performers on Santa Monica's Third Street Promenade, searching for an Internet café where we could get online. After some frantic searching, we read a police blotter about the triple murder from the night before. The attacker's ex-girlfriend and mother of his child had been in the house with our friends. She was shot first, then our friends. Three of the four had died. We sat in silence and disbelief, the café flooded with July sunlight.

During the ensuing period of grief, reflection, and mourning, I realized the extent to which I had previously been shielded from death. I had confronted it in the abstract only. Church and family had taught me that Christ triumphs over death, and death had been a central theme in college literature studies, but that had been death as a mere idea—in sermons, on the page, in classroom discussions. There's a maxim in the humanities: *Death is the mother of beauty.* In other words, without loss, without finitude, we wouldn't appreciate the beauty of transient things and relationships. This now seemed like a hollow abstraction. A triple homicide is certainly not the mother of beauty.

Living overseas, I had missed every death in my extended family, every funeral, every period of mourning, and I had felt those losses only in the most general terms. Death wasn't personal, just a story someone else told, but now all the deaths I had managed to avoid came flooding at me afresh. One grandparent from cancer. The other of Alzheimer's. Another quietly in the VA hospital. Each time, I hadn't been able to attend the funeral for one reason or another. The sudden deaths of friends my age opened up a space of grief within me—a period of attentiveness and acknowledgement of the unmourned deaths in my past, the individuals in my family who had died but also the relationships that had perished, the lost opportunities, the injuries to my own identity.

As I honored my grief, I also recognized that death has a valuable function in the spiritual life. From this perspective, death is not just an ending but also a new beginning. It marks a transition from one state to another. Christ taught, "Unless a grain of wheat dies, it remains alone, but if it dies, it bears much fruit" (John 12:24). In the months that followed my friends' deaths, I learned the necessity of moving through this uncomfortable process, cleansing myself from the past so that I could make space for new life.

Unprocessed deaths, I realized, can spread us thin. When we cling to aspects of the past for meaning, purpose, and identity, we are diminished, weakened, because our present is still determined by old fears, old wounds. Moving into the cave means identifying the things we need to let go, the things that have died—and then opening ourselves to this refining process, accepting the necessity of death for spiritual growth.

Something deep within us urges us along this path. The experience of death is painful, but we also have a sense of returning to something much deeper, something familiar that has been missing from our lives. We experience *nostalgia*, a word whose Greek root, *nostos*, means "homecoming," while *algos*, the other half of the word, means "pain, distress, grief"; *nostalgia* is the painful longing to go home.

The pattern of going home is central to the poems and stories of the great heroes. The epic poem of the ancient world, Homer's *Odyssey*, recounts the crafty Odysseus's twenty-year journey home to his island kingdom of Ithaca. There seems to be a universal *longing* for home underlying the ancient myths, and this is the kind of journey on which we too are about to embark. Like Odysseus and the other ancient heroes, we have a deep desire for home.

The word *desire* has its roots in *de sidere*—"from the stars."[1] Our desire for home is a celestial guiding force, similar to the way in which navigators once relied on the stars for direction. On Dante's journey through Hell, Purgatory, and Paradise in *The Divine Comedy*, he is constantly looking up at the stars, drawn to the heavens, oriented by them on his upward journey toward God.[2] This profound longing is what the various wisdom traditions call spiritual hunger and what the Eastern Christians called the movement toward theosis, or union with God, the ultimate goal of the spiritual journey.

But first, we must realize we're disoriented. That realization is what happened when we "woke up"—and at that point, we saw that the only path before us leads into the dark of the cave. This is where we stand now in our journey: in front of a craggy mouth into the rock. It's dark and damp inside, jagged and uninviting. Darkness means uncertainty; we don't know what we'll have to give up. We don't know what pain we'll have to face. But to experience the inner transformation on offer from the myths to the mystics, we understand this is the path we have to walk.

For most of us, this terrain produces anxiety. The cave represents our internal, often unconscious world, and this may be something we'd rather avoid. In the past, we've probably come up with all manner of escapes from it. But as the myths tell us, to identify our True Self and achieve a sense of integration, we have to descend into this foreboding darkness. We have to move down into a kind of spiritual death. In Matthew's Gospel, when Peter expresses the hope that Christ not have to suffer and die, Christ responds "Get behind me, Satan!" (Matthew 16:23). Commenting on this passage, author Henri Nouwen writes: "Living spiritually is made possible only through a direct, un-cushioned confrontation with the reality of death."[3]

In story after story, the saints in the Christian tradition, from the Desert Fathers and Mothers to Ignatius and Francis of Assisi, have literal experiences in caves, often following a point of conversion, signifying profound confrontation with the False Self. It is this territory into which we now move. Entering the cave and descending through the underworld is central to many myths.

The term for this downward movement on the spiritual journey is *katabasis*. Unlike mere death, the descent into the underworld is *katabasis* only if it is followed by a *return* from the underworld. The downward way implies the upward way; death anticipates a resurrection. In the *Odyssey*, Odysseus has to travel through the underworld, confronting many shades from his past, in order to learn how to get home from the blind seer Tiresias. For Dante, whose footsteps we are tracing in this book, the walk through Hell is the first part of his journey of discovery, which leads him back up Mount

Purgatory and to the heavenly spheres. In each of the mythic stories, the hero confronts the reality of death and suffering, both internally and externally, before achieving a sense of direction and renewal.

The real struggle is internal. This is an easy truth to gloss over, to parody even. Since the hero's journey has become a familiar pattern in film after film, from *Star Wars* to *Lion King*, from *The Lord of the Rings* to *Spider Man*, the invitation to journey inward can become a well-worn cliché.[4] We run the risk of dismissing the genuine reality of this essential opportunity for transformation.

It's easy to find excuses for avoiding the inner road. We don't like the dark—and we fear the death that lurks there: death of identity, of sustaining relationships, of access to our means of comfort. Stripped of our ego defenses, how will we fight the monsters waiting there for us? Without our usual weapons, our usual escape routes from pain, how will we engage with the world? What will we see and how will we cope with it?

In a sense, when it comes to this process, we are at a disadvantage over people in ages past. The natural cycles out of which many of the myths grew have become distant to us today. We live largely disconnected from Nature in urban and suburban developments, with artificial tree lines, artificial lawns, paved roads, air conditioning. Our technology, though providing the benefits of comfort and longer lives, has both tamed and muffled Nature and, by extension, what we can learn from it. The resulting loss of myth has removed traditional rites of passage that provide a means of confronting darkness, overcoming it, and acquiring agency and full adulthood, the recognition of full membership in the tribe or community. Instead, adolescence can drag on well into adulthood in our society, with a sense of helplessness, passivity, and victimization often taking the place of full maturity.

The primal truth we learn upon entering the cave is this: *the world is full of profound suffering.* This is the essence of the Christian notion of the Fall; it is also Buddha's realization that eventually led to his enlightenment. In the Judeo-Christian tradition, this is the fruit of the Tree of Knowledge of Good and Evil. The essence of wisdom is in how we respond to this central truth, but the first part of the spiritual journey is about confronting it fully.

Meanwhile, Western society is organized around the exchange of money for alleviating our suffering. Marketers imply that if we buy the right products, we'll finally eliminate our insecurity, our shortcomings, our inconveniences; we can push death back. This is the false edifice on which many of us build our collective lives, upon which our social fabric rests. We participate in a system that increasingly pulls a veil over our eyes, affecting our awareness, our consciousness, our desires, and our orientation. It determines *what* we see and *how* we see. In increasingly sophisticated ways, our basest desires are being manipulated. In some cases, we tacitly participate, and this process has become an accepted part of daily lives.

To take the step into the cave, to move onward and inward in spite of the fear, requires some sense of purpose, of desire for growth and movement. What we bring with us into the cave is our False Self, our ego. It is that which feels threatened. Our superficial identity—made out of our achievements, adornments, even our piety—has gotten us through daily life up until this point. We developed this identity early in childhood to survive, but it is mostly a fabrication, a construct. And it comes at a cost. Author Richard Rohr has identified several internal splits we make in creating our False Self: the split from our shadow self, allowing us to pretend to be our ideal self; the split of mind from body and soul, allowing us to hold ideals without living them; the split from death; and the split from others, allowing the illusion of superiority and status.[5]

Being transformed into full humanity and wisdom, according to the myths, requires giving ourselves over to a healthy form of death, one that removes our illusions and heals these disconnections. The first impulse, however, in confronting our inner self, in confronting death, in confronting suffering, is to retreat into the safety of this False Self. Acting out of unconsciousness increases when the ego and its needs feel threatened; we trumpet our status and achievements. We fear the exposure and the vulnerability that are the prerequisites for change. But to experience growth, we have to keep walking.

IMAGINE

Walk on. Feel the rock and sand underfoot. See the images flicker in the distance. What do you see up ahead? What will you have to confront here in the cave?

You take a deep breath, understanding you will leave something behind, understanding you will not walk away unscathed, understanding you will not walk away unchanged.

WAYPOST 1 EXERCISES

Select **at least two** exercises:

1. **Honoring Deaths:** List the major deaths you've experienced in your life so far (maybe of loved ones, a damaged relationship, an illness that forced you to let go

of your confidence in your own body, or a life change that brought an end to roles and relationships that were important to you). Are there deaths in your life you have not processed or honored? If it's the death of someone close to you, consider writing that person a letter of appreciation, or simply say good-bye in your own way. Light a candle and say a prayer. Maybe you can go to a place where you shared an important experience with this person and reconnect. If you're dealing with another sort of death, take the opportunity to honor this passing in your own way (write a poem, paint a picture, create a private ritual of farewell, journal, or simply allow yourself time and space to dwell on what has been lost).

2. **Life Chart:** List the following seven words on your page:

- work
- family/friendships
- creativity
- exercise
- play
- spirituality

Assign a percentage to each one, signifying how much time and energy you are able to devote to each in a given week. Is there an obvious imbalance? As you enter the "cave," consider what might need to change in your life in order to facilitate your journey. What might you need to release? Do you need to adjust the percentages you spend on each of these elements of life?

3. **Audio Divina:** Listen to a song that invokes waking up for you or dealing with personal pain. (My selection: "Comfortably Numb" covered by Dar Williams.)

4. **Poetica Divina:** Find the poem "The Waking" by Theodore Roethke. Read it through at least twice. Read it out loud. In your journal, describe how you've come to learn your most profound lessons. Were they from another person? An experience you had? How were you changed?

5. **Lectio Divina:** In Lectio Divina we want to have a direct encounter with a passage of Scripture. Rather than figuring out its meaning rationally, we let it speak to us here and now, engaging in *Reading, Reflection, Response*, and *Rest*, though these do not have to progress in a linear way. For this waypost, read Matthew 5:1–12 slowly. Then read the passage a second time, stopping to focus on any word, phrase, image, or impression that resonates with you.

Sit with the image or phrase, and allow it to speak to you. Respond inwardly to the message. Then read the passage slowly a third time before resting in silence, open to the unfolding of the passage in your heart.

NOTES

1. Dr. Thorpe notes here the findings of contemporary science: that our physical bodies are essentially stardust, and that the stars are therefore, quite literally, home.

2. In the highly ordered Aristotelian worldview, it is *desire* that keeps everything in motion, the spheres in their perfect celestial orbits moving according to their relationship to the Prime Mover. By Dante's time, this was integrated into the Christian worldview, with human desire, properly aligned by the will, tending toward God, and if distorted, tending toward other things.

3. Henri J. M. Nouwen.*Letters to Marc About Jesus* (New York: HarperCollins, 1998).

4. The pattern we recognize in these films is itself based on ancient world myths, catalogued and outlined by Joseph Campbell in *The Hero with a Thousand Faces*, and applied by screenwriting teachers like Christopher Vogler in *The Writer's Journey*. From obviously mythopoeic movies like *The Matrix* and the Harry Potter films, to more subtle uses in movies such as *Toy Story* and *Men in Black*, this pattern is ingrained in screenwriters, our modern mythmakers.

5. Richard Rohr. *The Naked Now: Learning to See as the Mystics See* (New York: Crossroad, 2009).

Are you willing to feel the pain of all the hurt that everyone has committed against everyone else in the world? We can fulfill the act of turning the poisonous feelings of anger, hatred, fury, rejection, despising, wanting to kill, wanting to die, and transform it into pure love. That requires forgiving. How many are willing to forgive on that level?

-SHUNYAMURTI

The Burning World

Waypost 2

As he walks into the darkness of the cave, Dante stays close to his guide. His first impression of Hell is the overwhelming noise: groans and loud cries, the sounds of anguish and rage. A naked throng of people are being stung and bitten by insects, their faces streaked with blood. Virgil explains that these are the souls of those who did not commit to either good or evil but rather lived their lives without making conscious moral choices. Both Heaven and Hell have denied them entry.

Virgil leads Dante to a great river called Acheron, which marks the border of Hell, where a crowd of newly dead souls waits to be taken across. Dante sees a boat approach, steered by an old man. When an earthquake suddenly shakes the ground, followed by a whirlwind and a thunderclap, Dante is so terrified that he faints. Meanwhile, the crowd frantically tries to climb aboard the ferryman's boat to cross the river, but only a select few make it aboard. The sights and sounds in the cave—the shrieks and the blood, the sheer volume of the damned—fills Dante with dread. He begins to weep.

Dante now begins his descent into the nine circles of Hell. He sees the souls receiving their just punishment, which always corresponds to their particular form of sin in life. Much of our religious notions of hell are filtered through the violence of this poem, so in a sense the terrain may seem familiar, but if we read the story mythically, symbolically (rather than as a literal description of hell) we gain insight into the ways in which our unhealthy patterns keep us in pain, keep us trapped.

On his journey, Dante encounters the lustful Paolo and Francesca, killed in their moment of passion by a vengeful husband and now blown about by eternal winds. He sees the souls of the gluttonous flayed and torn by the three-headed dog Cerberus, whose hunger is never satisfied. Wrathful souls tear and bite at each other's throats, while the sullen are buried in mud; they try to sing hymns but only gurgles emerge from their mouths. Those who committed suicide have been turned into trees that bleed black blood when broken, while others who were violent against God are burned by a rain of fire as they crawl across white hot sand. Demons whip panderers and seducers, and those who sold salvation for gold are turned upside down, their feet set on fire. Dante watches as historical figures such as Pope Nicholas III burn in a pit. Figures from mythology, like the monstrous Minotaur, chase Dante and Virgil, and they find biblical figures like Nimrod (who built the Tower of Babel) now buried in the walls of the lowest circle of Hell. Finally, Dante sees three traitors, Brutus, Cassius, and Judas, eternally gnawed by the giant figure of Lucifer encased in ice from the waist up, beating his wings, stirring up the freezing cold winds at the bottom of Hell.

IMAGINE

As you descend now on your own journey deeper into the cave, stumbling through the thick darkness, scenes from human history play out along the stone walls: volcanos burying cities in an instant; bodies frozen in glacial ice; floods drowning the innocent and the guilty alike; forest fires claiming father, mother, child; ancient intimate warfare with swords and spears, the battlegrounds slick with blood. You force yourself to fix your gaze on the unfolding scenes, and now you realize you are seeing more recent events: a mushroom cloud rising over Hiroshima, snuffing out tens of thousands of lives; hundreds of thousands of people starving to death in Ethiopia; millions of individuals dying from AIDS; giant waves heading landward as people try to flee, only to be caught in the immense undertow caused by the tsunami. The scenes seem to come faster and faster, and you are tempted to look away.

Not this time. You stop. You acknowledge. You bear witness.

Our world is like a mirror that reflects the images of the souls tormented in Dante's Hell. Often, like Dante, we find ourselves shrinking from the overwhelming suffering in the world. We build inner defense mechanisms to shield ourselves—but they offer only a temporary fix. When we don't face the realities of life, we stay tethered to our fears in a state of arrested development. We remain isolated, our anxieties easily triggered, constantly in a defensive posture. We may cut ourselves off from life and be easily overwhelmed by the many things onto which we project a sense of threat and danger. If we remain in this condition too long, we can succumb to despair. There is no escaping life's darkness.

This journey requires that we look squarely at the suffering in the world around us and within us—and come to terms with it. We would rather pretend the hellish pain and ugliness didn't exist, but coming to a new sense of balance and wholeness means we must face the darkness.

After graduating seminary and spending some time processing the death of my friends, I knew I wanted to engage in some kind of meaningful work, something that would put my gifts to use in direct service to others.

Such decisions, however well-intentioned, open us up further to the process of refinement. If, like I was, you are being guided to a work of service, you will encounter difficult realities: systemic injustice, suffering, violence, not to mention your own ego and toxic tendencies, your own limitations when it comes to bringing about meaningful and lasting change. If you've already been doing this kind of work, perhaps for many years, you may experience a deep sense of compassion fatigue; you may feel you've given all your energy without bringing about much change at all.

I worked for years as an aide in special education classrooms in the Pasadena public school system, where I was confronted firsthand with the after effects of segregation. The city's cultural reputation is that of wealth and status, but it also has a shadow side. One of the last cities in the country to integrate school systems, many of the mostly black and Hispanic students in my classes still lived in extreme poverty. Many of them had one or both parents in jail, or were raised by their grandmother, or were in foster care. Some suffered from mental health issues, and some were terminally ill. Almost all of them harbored deep wounds, resentments, and distrust. They needed something as simple as a kind word and encouragement, and they needed reliable structure for a sense of safety.

My students suffered from a wide range of disabilities, many of them caused by malnutrition in utero. One third grader had a debilitating bone and organ disease, and had to have a cup held in place next to his wheelchair in order to urinate. A set of autistic twins were given to violent outbursts whenever they were frustrated. Another student was a healthy fourth grader until he had three strokes that lamed the right side of his body; after that, his lunch had to be pureed, and he spoke by typing into a box.

My next job was as a high school teacher in downtown Los Angeles. One morning soon after my job there began, I noticed that a student from Guatemala had a vacant look and kept putting her head on her desk; she didn't respond to instructions or attempts at interaction from classmates, and when the bell rang, she didn't get up from her seat. When I asked her if she was okay, she burst into tears. The night before she had gotten a phone call that her mother, who had sent her to live with her uncle in America for a better life, had died from a heart attack.

Profound suffering is seldom very far away, and poverty exacerbates the problems. Crime rates are not the only areas of concern; children often have scant access to nutritious food, and their incidence of asthma and other medical conditions is high. All residents of poor communities are at higher risk for cancer, heart disease, and diabetes. In the face of such overwhelming suffering, we are tempted to take shelter once again in our defense mechanisms: Numbness. Distraction. Busyness. Cynicism. Platitudes. Maybe even a sense of exception and privilege.

But even here in this dark reality, there are insights to be gained: for one thing, the value of this short gift of life, tenuous, fragile, brief. In privileged circles, we can construct our lives to buffer us, to shield us from suffering. Most of us do not choose to be callous or apathetic but pursue lives that directly or indirectly help us avoid suffering, both in ourselves and in others. And on the surface, it makes sense. Why would we actively seek out suffering? We all have our distractions: work, TV, video games, self-improvement, cell phones, resort vacations, careers. Most of these aren't evil in and of themselves, of course. But we can end up becoming consumed by them, walled off. Instead, this journey calls us to a space of intentional encounter and to witness suffering with our defenses lowered.

This process of confronting suffering is a central part of the mythic journey. After his baptism and experience of calling, Christ does not begin his work immediately. Instead he goes into the wilderness to confront temptation, becoming equipped to see through to the suffering of beggars, prostitutes, tax collectors, and thieves. In mythic terms, this downward journey is a necessary part of learning how to become whole, of learning how to get to an internal state of home, as well as how to act in the world out of that wholeness. The image of the crucifixion has such a lasting hold on the imagination because it represents a Christ in his compassion who suffers with us, understanding full well the very real pain that entails.

IMAGINE

As you journey downward, what scenes play out now on the walls of the cave? Do you see the mass graves;

people in chains; lynchings lit by a burning cross, the symbol of grace and redemption distorted; bodies riddled with gunfire, bloodied with knife wounds, or torn apart by bombs? Do you recognize yourself in the suffering faces—or do they seem "other," unfamiliar because their skin is another shade than yours or their beliefs and cultures seem strange? So often we perceive "the other" not as a child of God like us, not as one from whom we can learn, someone we need, for whom we are also responsible, but as an enemy—of our faith, our country, our ideology. These so-called "aliens" may come to represent in some way an obstacle to our own goals. Can you see past these mental discriminations now (including the ones you keep hidden, perhaps even from yourself), and perceive yourself as united with the pain you observe? If so, the artificial barrier you've erected around yourself disappears, and you share in the world's agony.

You descend further and come to level ground. Here you again see images moving across the wall from the centuries of Earth's history, but now time no longer seems to separate you from these long-ago scenes of destruction and despair. The suffering you see is yours; you are both the victim and the perpetrator of violence. You share in the world's eons of violence and torment.

As you watch, the medieval crusaders move across the European continent like locusts, leaving devastation in their wake even before they reach their destination. Once they reach Jerusalem, they slaughter, rape, and pillage through the streets of the Holy City. In the shadows, you see someone sitting against the cave wall, and as you move closer, you hear him describe some of what he saw on the day he and his companions attacked the city:

> Soon all the defenders were leaving the walls and running through the city, pursued by our men, who drove them along, cutting them down and following them as far as the Temple of Solomon, where there was such a blood-bath that our men were wading ankle deep in blood. Soon the crusaders were rushing through the whole city, seizing gold, silver, horses and mules and looting the houses that were full of costly things. Then, happy and indeed weeping for joy, our men went to venerate and pray at the sepulchre of our Redeemer. [1]

Walking on, you see more images from history. This time, enemies of church and state are being burned at the stake: now the Catholic, now the Protestant, now the Jew, now the woman accused of witchcraft. Whatever their "crime," they are each and all the Eternal Other, separated from mainstream society by their heretical beliefs, heretical writings, heretical politics, heretical skin color, or heretical gender. As you watch, body after body turns to ash and smoke.

As you continue you, you see that a monk is seated here, wearing a brown habit with a simple cord for a belt, his head tonsured. A faint scent of dust and smoke clings to him. Moving closer, you hear him describing the conditions in the Americas after the arrival of the Europeans:

The tyranny exercised by the Spaniards against the Indians in the work of pearl fishing is one of the most cruel that can be imagined. There is no life as infernal and desperate in this century that can be compared with it. . . . The pearl fishers dive into the sea at a depth of five fathoms, and do this from sunrise to sunset, and remain for many minutes without breathing, tearing the oysters out of their rocky beds where the pearls are formed. They come to the surface with a netted bag of these oysters where a Spanish torturer is waiting in a canoe or skiff, and if the pearl diver shows signs of wanting to rest, he is showered with blows, his hair is pulled, and he is thrown back into the water, obliged to continue the hard work of tearing out the oysters and bringing them again to the surface. . . . At night the pearl divers are chained so they cannot escape. Often a pearl diver does not return to the surface, for these waters are infested with man-eating sharks of two kinds, both vicious marine animals that can kill, eat, and swallow a whole man. And it is solely because of the Spaniards' greed for gold that they force the Indians to lead such a life, often a brief life, for it is impossible to continue long diving into the water and holding the breath for minutes at a time, repeating this for hour after hour, day after day; the continual cold penetrates them, constricts the chest, and they die spitting blood, or weakened by diarrhea.[2]

The suffering settles over you, mind and body, layer upon layer. As you move on past the monk, the shade of another man flickers into life. He is black, his manner calm and measured; you notice the marks around his wrists and ankles. His voice is low and raspy as he tells about his passage from Africa:

The closeness of the place, and the heat of the climate, added to the number in the ship, which was so crowded that each had scarcely room to turn himself, almost suffocated us. This produced copious perspirations, so that the air soon became unfit for respiration, from a variety of loathsome smells, and brought on a sickness among the slaves, of which many died, thus falling victims to the improvident avarice, as I may call it, of their purchasers. This wretched situation was again aggravated by the galling of the chains, now become insupportable; and the filth of the necessary tubs, into which the children often fell, and were almost suffocated. The shrieks of the women, and the groans of the dying, rendered the whole a scene of horror almost inconceivable. [3]

You shudder as you listen, and then another man steps out of the shadows and tells his story in a low voice:

It is a common custom, in the part of Maryland from which I ran away, to part children from their mothers at a very early age. Frequently, before the child has reached its twelfth month, its mother is taken from it, and hired out on some farm a considerable distance off, and the child is placed under the care of an old woman, too old for field labor. For what this separation is done, I do not know, unless it be to hinder the development of the child's affection toward its mother, and to blunt and destroy the natural affection of the mother for the child. This is the inevitable result.

I never saw my mother, to know her as such, more than four or five times in my life; and each of these times was very short in duration, and at night. She was hired by a Mr. Stewart, who lived about twelve miles from my home. She made her journeys to see me in the night, travelling the whole distance on foot, after the performance of her day's work. She was a field hand,

and a whipping is the penalty of not being in the field at sunrise, unless a slave has special permission from his or her master to the contrary—a permission which they seldom get, and one that gives to him that gives it the proud name of being a kind master. I do not recollect of ever seeing my mother by the light of day. She was with me in the night. She would lie down with me, and get me to sleep, but long before I waked she was gone. Very little communication ever took place between us. Death soon ended what little we could have while she lived, and with it her hardships and suffering. She died when I was about seven years old, on one of my master's farms, near Lee's Mill. I was not allowed to be present during her illness, at her death, or burial. She was gone long before I knew any thing about it.[4]

The man falls silent, and you walk on. The visions on the stone walls are from your own time now, you realize, though these are realities you have distanced yourself from: villagers' daughter sold to pay off family debt; children in factories sewing clothes to be sold in America and Europe; trafficked children, their hooded shadows in the back of a truck. In each of these grim visions, you see that humans have refused to see the Other as a fellow creature. We are capable of this destruction and savagery, you realize, of sinking into the tragic logic of the blood feud—but you can no longer separate yourself from those who have committed these atrocities, for you understand now that you are also capable of the same violence and cruelty. As you watch the centuries of human horror play out on the cave walls, you know you are seeing the ghastly distortion of what Genesis calls our "Divine image." You are observing firsthand the parade of egos across the years, False Selves strutting and pontificating, while they dehumanize each other in order to justify their selfishness and brutality.

Part of our difficulty in coming to terms with the violence and suffering in the world is our lack of understanding about its source. Instead, we give it a label and distance ourselves from it. It's external, "out there." We project the evil and savagery onto others (it's always "them" who are at fault, never "us"). Meanwhile, we fail to see the ways in which we helped create the conditions for suffering, the ways in which we continue to contribute to its reality.

When we cling to what is good for us alone, both as a society (or nation) and as individuals, we find ourselves in competition with those around us for money, for attention, for power, for affection, for control. Even if we expand our sense of identity beyond our individual interests and invest it into our community—or tribe or church or organization—we often cling to our sense of pride in our separation, our differences, our so-called superiority. We look for ways in which others threaten us, antagonize us; we notice all the things that offend us, and in doing so, we consolidate our sense of righteousness. We prove to ourselves over and over that *we're right* and *they're wrong*. "They" become the scapegoats for all that's wrong in our lives.

Rigid categories take shape in our minds: who's in and who's out (who is like us and who is different). In the process, those same mental categories bring about the divisions that often end in violence. There's always someone to fight. And if we defeat them, the mental category of *enemy* doesn't go away; we'll soon find someone else to fill the slot.

Our journey requires that we unearth and examine the distortions within our own hearts and minds—and that we be able to see the ways in which they have helped support external conflicts. Once we see this distortion at work in ourselves, we are more able to extend grace and compassion in the face of unconscious anger and hostility in others. Rooted in awareness of ourselves, we can contribute more effectively to peace and wholeness. If, however, we are buried in unconscious egocentrism, we will inevitably contribute to the problem. Pain breeds pain.

Early in childhood, we all developed strategies to cope with pain and our sense of lack. At the same time, usually between the ages of four and eight, we absorbed the additional layers of family and cultural conditioning. These thought patterns become so deeply ingrained as to be nearly invisible to us. On the surface, we may consider ourselves to be enlightened, progressive, compassionate people, never realizing that we are all the while functioning with an old operating system.

This was brought home to me in a very personal way when the details of my high school friends' deaths came out several years later, during media coverage of the trial of the man accused in the shooting.

The woman on the telephone . . . pleaded with a 911 dispatcher. "I'm in apartment 10 on Fourth Street. . . Please, help me," she said before the line went dead. This was the assailant's girlfriend, one of three people executed that night by a man who broke into the condominium looking for her. The 911 recording was played Wednesday in the sentencing of the defendant, who pleaded guilty in June to capital murder and other charges. Prosecutors asked the Judge to impose the death penalty against the defendant, who they said moved methodically from one victim to another, firing his handgun at the heads of the group of people who had been waiting for pizza that Memorial Day weekend. When the rampage was over, three were dead, including the mother of his daughter. Two were wounded. The woman was found in the hallway outside the apartment, near her cellular phone. The smell of gunpowder lingered as police forced their way inside, according to one of the first officers on scene. One of the victims was lying over a bowl of potato chips he was carrying; another was dead on a sofa. One of two survivors testified that she encountered the assailant standing in a bedroom. He had used a car key to slice open the window screen. "You're going to be the first to die," the assailant said as he held the .45-caliber semiautomatic handgun to her head. He shot her once each in the chest, jaw, and arm. She testified that a bullet is still lodged in her chest. The assailant moved to another room and found a victim. "Shoot me and please just go away," he told the assailant. "This isn't like the movies or anything," the shooter responded before firing. The victim survived.

I experienced an immediate visceral response as I read this account of my friends' assault, and I imagined how the parents must feel as they read the details of their children's deaths. "Where does healing come from?" I wondered. "How do we move toward wholeness?" There was no miraculous healing salve I could prescribe, no phrase or Bible verse that would lessen the suffering of my friends' families. Maybe they were softened by their pain and found a deeper capacity for compassion. Or maybe they became walled off, bitter, and distrustful. I don't know.

I do know that when we or those we care about have been victimized, it's all too easy to demonize the perpetrator (either as an individual or as a group). Then, just as pain begets pain, violence often begets more violence. When we are in pain, we may be tempted to summon moral indignation in our defense, using it to isolate evil as a quality only in others, rather than facing its reality in ourselves. When we take that route, suffering can become a means of consolidating our ego identity. It can be something we wrap ourselves up in, something we use as a shield—or wield as a weapon. In so doing, we often perpetuate the problem. Division and a propensity to violence escalates, both in ourselves and in our world. We must widen our lens in order to see beyond our barriers, so that we can reach a deeper understanding of the seeds of violence.

Part of the process of transformation that Dante's journey asks of us is to attend to the suffering in others, listening to their stories, hearing their voices. This awakens a connective response in us, allowing us to make a compassionate turn away from selfishness. Paying attention to others' stories, whether from a long time ago or right now, has a decentering effect; it takes us out of our own heads. It allows us a moment to let go of our own struggles, our own preoccupations, and see the reality of others as though they were ourselves.

Once we have allowed that to happen, we need to also do the even harder work of looking deeply into our own suffering—the inner work of identifying our own anguish, our own ego strategies, and our own violence. It's not enough to cry for justice and identify with the victim, which is our normal response. Growing toward wholeness means also identifying with the pain of the victimizer.

This does not excuse the action. But if the world is burning (and it is), it is because we are burning. Every day brings new opportunities to find something to cling to, a position to stake out, an identity to claim, and this leads to defensiveness, aggression, violence. Violence is an unskillful, broken response to pain—and the world is full of pain. How we deal with our own pain dictates whether we will contribute to the world's violence or help transform it.

IMAGINE

Here in the cave, the images begin to fade now. Take a deep breath and feel your way forward. In the distance, there seems to be a faint light. Slowly, you make your way toward it.

WAYPOST 2 EXERCISES

Select **at least two** exercises:

1. **The Other:** Our natural tendency is to identify with the suffering in these stories, but getting at the root of suffering means identifying how and why we must also identify with the person or persons who caused the suffering. How do we too exclude others, look down on others, mistreat others, ignore others? Write in your journal at least two kinds of people or groups you view as *other*, based on their gender, sexual orientation, politics, religious beliefs, nationality or ethnicity, their job, or their neighborhood. Think about whom you would be uncomfortable inviting to your home for dinner. Whom would you be reluctant to welcome into the family? Whom are you likely to make fun of—or merely dismiss or

ignore? What characteristics make you think less of a person? Physical appearance? Political beliefs? Criminal background? Level of education? Personal habits, such as smoking or annoying mannerisms? Religious beliefs (whether more conservative, more liberal, or entirely different from your own)? As part of this exercise, imagine a particular individual from one of these groups. Give the person a back-story. Write a short description of the kind of life that created the conditions for this person becoming who they are today.

2. **The Catalyst:** What person in your life has inspired you the most to cultivate compassion for others? How so?

3. **Audio Divina:** Listen to a song that invokes the suffering world for you. (My selections: "Strange Fruit" by Billy Holiday, "Keep on Rocking in the Free World" by Neil Young, "Sunday Bloody Sunday" by U2.)

4. **Poetica Divina:** Read the poem "Death Fugue" by Paul Celan and look up online Anselm Kiefer's paintings *Shulamith, Märkische Heide,* and *Margarete.* Research the connections between the paintings and the poem. What response is evoked in you?

5. **Moral Inventory:** In what ways are you dishonest with yourself? Conduct a brutally honest moral inventory. What things about yourself do you try to hide or sweep under the rug? If appropriate, share these with someone this week.

6. **Lectio Divina:** Psalm 74 (Read, Reflect, Respond, Rest).

NOTES

1. From the *Gesta Francorum*, author anonymous, pub. 1101.

2. From *A Short Account of the Destruction of the Indies*, Bartolome de las Casas, pub. 1552.

3. From An *Interesting Narrative of the Life of Oloudah Equiano*, Oloudah Equiano, pub. 1789.

4. From *A Narrative of the Life of Frederick Douglass*, Frederick Douglass, pub. 1845.

Nothing has a stronger effect psychologically on their environment and especially on their children than the unlived life of the parent.

-C.J. JUNG

Everyone carries a parental wound and has a wounded parent. But through wounding we enter a crossroads, between innocence and maturity, from a superficial life to penetrating awareness.

-JAMES HILLMAN

The Burning House

Waypost 3

As Dante enters the ninth circle of Hell, he sees the shades of those who have committed violence against family encased in ice up to their faces. Their teeth chatter and their tears freeze instantly, forcing their eyes shut. Blind, caring little for anyone else and showing no remorse for the harm they've caused in life, the shades ask Dante to take the names of their fellow prisoners back to the upper world to damage their reputations and ruin their family names. This is fitting for those who commit violence by betraying family. Even in the afterlife they look to harm those close to them. They are cunning and vicious and threatening, even as their entire bodies are frozen. Their desire to inflict pain extends even into the afterlife.

For Dante, family bonds are so sacred that some of the lowest spheres of Hell are reserved for those who violate them. In these passages, the poet acknowledges the depth of the wounds we receive from family. These wounds damage not only ourselves but also society as a whole. This kind of treachery, Dante indicates, undermines the very fabric of the social order.

IMAGINE

As you continue now on your path deeper into the bowels of the cave, jagged rocks clutter the path, and in the darkening haze, it's difficult to see where to place your feet. You have a growing sense of unease. A flickering light grows brighter ahead of you, and then you emerge into a wide level area. In the dim light, you see a narrow stream running through the cavern. An old house stands in the shadows, a fire blazing beside it. Shadowy figures move through the gloom. Some sit by the stream in silence, while others wander alone. Others sit and talk, sharing stories and laughter.

As you walk deeper into this mythical space, you begin the work of uncovering the wounds and destructive patterns that are rooted in your family of origin.

We move now from our focus on the suffering in the world to an awareness of family suffering. To look deeply into our own destructive habits, we need to understand the context in which they were formed, and no influence is greater than the family system in which we grew up. Here is where our identities were established; here is where we deeply internalized who we still think we are today. The roles we continue to play were born and perpetuated within our families of origin. This is where our core wounds were inflicted, and it's where we established our patterns of defensive coping and compensating. The False Self was born here. When family members don't work toward becoming conscious of their own patterns, the danger is even greater that we'll perpetuate the cycle of unconsciousness.

In the ancient Greek myths, the House of Atreus was a family divided by violence. To appease the gods and guarantee his ships' safe passage to Troy, King Agamemnon of Mycenae sacrificed his daughter, Iphigenia. When he returned from the war ten years later after a hard-won victory, his wife, Clytemnestra, and her lover, Aegisthus, conspired to kill King Agamemnon to avenge Iphigenia's death. Then Agamemnon's son Orestes is duty bound to avenge his father's death by killing the murderers, thus perpetuating the vicious cycle. His act of vengeance complete, the Furies, mythical forces of divine retribution, hunt down Orestes and torment him.[1]

Stories like these are not unique to Greek mythology. In the Hebrew scriptures, the story of the Patriarchs (Abraham, Isaac, and Jacob) are shot through with family conflict, violation, retribution, and redemption. Abraham is willing to sacrifice his son Isaac on Mount Moriah; Jacob is in conflict with his brother Esau; and Jacob's son, Joseph, is sold into slavery by his brothers. These stories make clear that the family has always been the source of our deepest wounds.

The wounds we suffer from family life are of course wide and varied. We can be unwanted. We can be neglected. We can be physically or sexually abused. We can be verbally abused or internalize unspoken tensions in the household. We can experience jealousy and rejection from parents who feel we've taken away the affection and attention they once received from their partners. We can be left with the scars of a broken family, feeling responsible for contributing to the conflict and separation; even very young children blame themselves for being unable to hold the family together.

When we are children, our family is the universe. It mediates the world to us. We build our understanding of how the world works, what people will expect, what dangers exist, and how to define success or failure from this early experience. Whether we were idealized by a parent and could do no wrong or felt almost invisible, early family life shapes our orientation to others and the world around us. It affects our sense of personal value and competence. It influences how we expect to be treated by others as adults and how we engage in relationships.

One of the factors contributing to our core wounds, and one over which we have no control whatsoever, is our birth order, which so strongly influences how we understand the world on a gut level and how we interact with our environment. Today there are all different kinds of family structures, but even "traditional" nuclear families are emotionally complex; regardless of the particulars of the family structure, birth order and the way in which we are received into the family structure has a lasting effect on our self-understanding.

These factors often determine the roles we adopt unconsciously throughout our lives. Older siblings can be tasked with more responsibility and may grow up looking out for others, or they may become resentful if leaned on too heavily; they may also grow up with a stronger ability for initiative and influence. Middle children may have a longer identity crisis, or a stronger need for stability, since their status was displaced and their world disrupted at a young age by the birth of a sibling; they may be combative because they feel they have to fight for attention. The youngest may feel emotionally unfulfilled in spite of attention and adoration; maybe the parents had little emotional energy left after having multiple kids already. Whatever our birth order, it will help determine how much power we feel we have to influence those around us. Our attitudes and expectations will in turn shape how we are viewed and how we are treated.

I am the youngest in a family of five, with strong personalities in the household, so the family values, dynamics, and identities were fairly fixed by the time I was born. As the youngest, I often felt I had little say in family decisions. The family system was patriarchal, meaning that even as I received ample praise, attention, and affection, my influence was still more limited. As a result, I've often experienced the world as largely predetermined, with rules, processes, roles, and identities beyond the family also fairly fixed, leaving me with a reduced sense of agency or ability to influence any kind of change in my environment. So strong was the power of this lens through which I viewed the world, I was years into adulthood before I felt I could do anything that might make a difference. I was raised in a loving, stable, supportive home, but like any family system, it left each of its members with unique obstacles to overcome.

Tensions, lingering resentments, unconscious fears, infighting, and power struggles are par for the course in family systems, no matter how outwardly stable they may appear to be. Often, great suffering is inflicted by parents who have also greatly suffered. Hurt people hurt people, and large-scale suffering is deeply rooted in individual suffering. Family is the primary crucible for that pain.

If we want to understand our home life, its particular shape, its griefs, its taboos, its capacity for support, its warmth or coldness, its demands, its areas of accountability, its fears, its power dynamics, and its emotional land mines, we have to look at our parents' wounds. The core needs of the parents have a deep impact on the entire family.

At seventeen, my mom suffered a series of blows in short order: her parents separated, she was violated on a date, and she became pregnant. Despite her mother's urging, she refused to use the child as a means to persuade her father to come back, and as a result, her mother rejected her. During the pregnancy, my mother moved several times, finally moving in with her father. When the baby boy was born, she placed him into adoption. At the time, most adoptions were closed, and so she knew nothing of him for many years. My mother had undoubtedly suffered other wounds prior to this, since her father had drank heavily after his discharge from the service, but those wounds were consolidated and intensified by this powerful experience of victimization, then rejection, followed by the heartsick grief of placing her first-born son into adoption, and finally her deep and lasting sense of shame. Several years later, she became a follower of Jesus, and soon after that, she met and married a young man with a secure belief system from an intact home who accepted her for who she was. She took her faith very seriously, and that, combined with her relationship with my father, provided context and relief from her pain. But her wounds remained. She raised her three other sons; she showed great compassion and forgiveness for both her parents later in life, and she cared for her mother in her old age—but she also struggled with her sense of identity and with bouts of depression. Her childhood wounds gave her an intense need for an emotionally stable environment, and any perceived threat to family stability required immediate attention. At her deepest, most primitive core, she had learned that family upheaval meant great suffering. Her anxiety surrounding this need for stability could create situations that felt frustratingly stifling. Through no fault of her own, her wounds became my wounds, at least to some extent.

Meanwhile, my father's story was shaped by growing up in the poorest family on the street. His father had been a sergeant in World War II and was known for his kindness, his work ethic, and his integrity, but he never had much of a formal education and returned from the war to drive a laundry truck in a small town. The income was meager, their family existence humble. My father and his four siblings wore the shabbiest clothes on the block, played with the oldest toys, and made do with what little they had. This would not have been so bad if the other children on their block had not passed around a petition for them to move somewhere else. The oldest boy in the group took the petition to my grandparents' house, rang the doorbell, and then handed it to my grandmother. My dad still remembers the look of pain on his mother's face when she read the petition for her family to leave the neighborhood.

This incident, perhaps combined with my father's birth order and role in the family, as well as a combination of other experiences, gave my dad a profound need for security and stability. Rather than seeking to exert control over his physical environment, this need manifests for him in an attempt to bring about moral stability, integrity, and consistency. He brings this to his work as a husband, father, pastor, and mentor to younger pastors. Those who share a need for stability tend to feel safe in his presence or under his leadership.

Deep wounds can help to create strengths, as well as weaknesses, and parents cannot help but share both with their children. My upbringing was warm, caring, and supportive, but we sometimes also fell into the pattern of sacrificing emotional honesty if it meant preserving domestic stability. A core need for stability and security is neither inherently good nor inherently bad, but leaving it unexamined and unearthed can keep us mired in unhealthy or even destructive patterns.

The way in which we internalize and live out our parents' core wounds corresponds to what the Christian tradition calls *original sin*. These deep-seated fears limit who we are and how we live. They create an internal dissonance, an inner distortion; they cause us to look for happiness in the wrong places. They form the roots of the False Self.

Whatever our core wounds may be, we too will pass these on to our children through our worries, our fears, our praise, and our punishment. If left unexamined, they in turn will pass them on to their children as well. Sometimes, children will overcompensate and pass along tendencies that go to the opposite extreme. In either case, insight, awareness, and understanding are needed for us to move toward wholeness, and in so doing, become agents of wholeness.

For that to happen, we have to face our own shadows, our own shame, our own fear, our own wounds. This shadowy realm is the space that sets our boundaries;

it is the place where we live out much of our lives; and yet it is also the space we avoid most, the space we go to great lengths to keep hidden from our friends and our families, from our partners and even ourselves. To find growth, to find maturity, to find our true homes, we have to explore that space.

What we seek in this part of the journey is encounter, confrontation, awareness, and clarity, even if that requires some amount of pain. In fact, at this point we need to identify specific areas of pain, the precise wounds whose scars we still bear—memories of a careless word spoken by a family member, for example, moments of rejection, or conflicts never quite resolved but merely swept under the rug.

Therapists often encourage patients to reflect on their mother wounds or father wounds—core needs that were left unmet and that continue to shape their lives as adults. Sometimes core addictions can be traced back to an absence, distance, or lack of intimacy with a same-sex or opposite-sex parent. The mother function, for example, is to empower, to nurture, to protect, and to initiate, but each of us faced our unique obstacles in these areas, which can contribute to self-limiting beliefs, learned helplessness, a victim identity, or other problems. A professional setting with a trained therapist may be necessary to identify these issues and move past them.

We may feel deeply resentful of the pain or limitations caused by family dynamics; after all, we had no say in what our parents passed down to us. As we continue on our journey, however, walking the path Dante has left for us, we will be able to heal our limited ego—our small, wounded self—far more effectively if we can open ourselves to a deeper awareness of our parents' pain, remembering that they too inherited their pain. They too were once innocent children who had no power to control the dynamics of their own families of origin.

This level of compassionate understanding is quite different from identifying with our childhood wounds. Wrapping ourselves in the pain of our personal beginnings—whether it stems from our culture, community, or family—only breeds a sense of victimhood and possibly entitlement. It can make us believe we are powerless and can prevent us from growing. Instead, as we look squarely at this suffering, directing an unbroken gaze toward it, we separate ourselves from it. It is there, it is real, but it is not *us*. Stepping back from the pain allows us to find our true identities, while it expands our ability for compassion and understanding.

There are other, less helpful options for dealing with family wounds, however. Some of us gloss over our families' shortcomings, while at the same time we over-romanticize their virtues, their nobility, or their achievements. This refusal to take a clear-eyed, accurate look at our childhood is often rooted in a need to overcome a sense of smallness, powerlessness, or worthlessness. Our egos long for exceptionalism.

Parents may demonstrate this need by projecting it onto their children, exaggerating their accomplishments and abilities. This can cause its own kind of resentment and pain, since it may demand that we live up to impossible ideals, compromising honesty and authenticity to maintain the family roles and identity, whatever that may be (athletes or musicians, artists or academics, professionals or "working folk," atheists or "good Christians").

To cope with the sense of lack we feel inside, some of us find a substitute or extended family system in our work, ideology, nationality, or faith community. To bolster our own inadequacy, we over-identify with a group that has traits we admire. This is usually an unconscious process that can contribute to our unacknowledged prejudices—who's in, who's out; who's good, who's bad; who's deserving, who isn't—as we identify evil as existing only outside our narrow circle, while we fail to acknowledge our own capacity for it. We develop a highly selective story about some other group, and then we project our fears and insecurities onto it. This perpetuates the cycle of the broken identity, the False Self, the judgmental ego.

Whatever combination of wounds and faulty conditioning we carry from our family systems—and we all do to one degree or another—our understanding of the ego center's needs can provide a helpful framework for uncovering unhealthy patterns and brokenness. According to Thomas Keating, who wrote a great deal about the False Self versus the True Self, human beings tend to struggle with three dominant needs that become deeply ingrained in our unconscious and become organizing principles in our life choices: the need for *stability and security*, the need for *affection and esteem*, and the need for *power and control*.[2] We have each of these needs to varying degrees but usually one is dominant, corresponding to a painful experience or withholding in early childhood, usually between the ages of one and three. We'll explore this in more depth in the next chapter, but applying this concept to our parents can be helpful at this stage of our journey.

People who have a need for stability and security, as my parents did, seek to find that both for themselves and for those close to them. This can be both comforting and oppressive for the family, depending on how the need manifests itself and how other family members receive it. Those with a need for affection and esteem can be attentive and comforting but also overly sensitive and needy. Those with a need for power and control can be protective and strong but also cold and callous.

Take a moment to consider:

- What did your parents' core needs tend to be?
- How did that affect the home?
- Where did these needs come from in their own homes of origin? What did your parents experience? What lack did they compensate for?
- How did that affect how they organized their later lives, their needs, habits, and tendencies?
- How did they grow over time?

I am not offering this direction as a point of fixation; we need not be immobilized like insects in amber by whatever strengths or weaknesses our parents brought to the family. Instead, this is a place to pause in our journey and take some time to examine our parents' suffering. In doing so, we not only gain greater freedom for ourselves, but we also develop a greater compassionate awareness in general. Then, as we become aware of the unconscious hang-ups we carry because we are looking through the lens of our parents' experiences, we can begin to let go of these false assumptions and move on toward a greater wholeness.

IMAGINE

Before you descend further, you linger beside the fire here in this cavern. You take some time to listen to the family stories being told by the people who are gathered there. As you listen, you realize these are familiar voices; your parents, your grandparents, and your ancestors from even farther back in time are all here, sharing the experiences that are your own heritage.

As the voices finally fall silent, you leave the fireside and enter the house. Inside, you find rooms you remember from your childhood: the kitchen, the living room, the bedrooms of the home where you grew up. The furniture is dusty, the walls festooned with cobwebs, and the air is filled with the odor of mildew. After you have looked around, venturing into each of the familiar rooms, you get out a broom and a mop, roll up your sleeves, and begin to clean.

While you work, you reflect on the emotions that linger in your memory in each of these rooms—your family's common sources of tension and conflict, spoken or unspoken; the power dynamics that were in play; what your family valued; and what your parents feared. Pay attention to the emotions that arise. Let moments of family conflict come to your mind, moments of crisis, of rage, of grief, and of fear, as well as of gratitude, contentment, and joy. Remember, you no longer live here. You can observe these emotions and events from the outside. See them, pay attention to them—and let them pass. Here in the cave, we seek awareness, not judgment; understanding, not revenge.

When you are ready, look around the rooms one more time—and then go out the door and close it behind you. Continue on your way.

WAYPOST 3 EXERCISES

Select **at least two** exercises:

1. **The House:** Write a description of the house you spent the most time in while you were growing up. If you moved around a lot, describe what each place where you lived had in common (perhaps the furniture, the way the kitchen was organized, or your toys). Pay attention to the images and memories that bubble up as you write.

2. **Visio Divina:** Spend some time with family photos this week if you have them. What memories come up for you? Maybe it's simple gratitude. Maybe you're more keenly aware of some of the challenges a family

member has faced. Reflect. Consider reaching out with a note of encouragement if the individuals are still alive, or a prayer of some kind if they're not.

3. **The Wound:** Write a letter to the family member whose wounds affected you the most. What do you most need to express? (You don't need to actually send the letter.)

4. **Family Dynamics:** What support and nurturing did your family of origin provide? How did it fall short of the ideal? What family dynamics were most limiting to growth, health, and wholeness? List three nurturing and three limiting elements in your family system and write about your role in the dynamic. How do these elements continue to affect your life today?

5. **Audio Divina:** Listen to a song that invokes for you either the family wound or the redeemed family. (My selections: "Mother" by John Lennon, "Dear Father" by Colin Hay, "Sometimes You Can't Make It on Your Own" by U2, "Mercy Street" by Peter Gabriel, "Heavenly Father" by Bon Iver.) Does the song trigger any strong emotional reactions or memories? Consider wounds from your family that have come to define

who you are. What wounds have you held on to? Which ones have influenced your identity and your decisions in life? Write a journal entry in response to the music.

6. **Poetica Divina:** Read "Those Winter Sundays" by Robert Hayden. Look up the phrase "liturgy of the hours" as well and consider the possible different meanings of the word "offices" at the end of the poem. Read the poems "A Litany" and "Gathering Up the Bones" by Gregory Orr. Notice your emotional response to these poems, and write in your journal any memories that come to mind.

7. **Lectio Divina:** Genesis 45:1–15 (Read, Reflect, Respond, *Rest*).

NOTES

1. This myth has echoed down through the centuries, serving as the basis for Shakespeare's *Hamlet*, and later Disney's *The Lion King*. This is one example of the way myths stay timeless, by treating universal issues of growing up and confronting core conflicts in the family, for example.

2. Thomas Keating. *The Human Condition* (Mahwah, NJ: Paulist Press, 1999), pages 13–14.

The heart of the Christian ascesis [discipline] is the struggle with our unconscious motivations. If we do not recognize and confront the hidden influences of the emotional programs for happiness, the False Self will adjust to any new situation in a short time and nothing is really changed.

-THOMAS KEATING

What God does—what life does—is gradually destabilize the supposed boundaries of the small self so we can awaken inside of the Large Self, which we call God. This usually happens through experiences of great love or great suffering or inner prayer journeys that allow the private ego to collapse back into the True Self, who we are in God.

-RICHARD ROHR

The Burning Self

Waypost 4

As Dante moves ever lower through the rings of Hell, through swamps and lakes of fire, he is terrified of the beasts that block his way. He turns pale when demons obstruct his path, so scared that he even resists his guide Virgil. Ashamed at his own lack of understanding throughout his life, he faints when he hears how two lovers' adulterous desire was fanned into flame by a medieval romance, because he himself stokes desire in his own writing; he realizes he is complicit in the fall of others. The sight of the contorted bodies of the diviners, astrologers, and magicians, whose heads have been twisted and are forced to walk backward, makes him weep. The sheer scale of the suffering he sees overwhelms him, and his guide needs to correct and encourage him over and over again. In some sense, the downward way for Dante is about the recognition of his own fear and shame, his own complicity in and capacity for corruption. His journey is one of profound self-discovery.

And then Dante comes to the frozen bottom of Hell, where he sees Lucifer himself, encased up to the waist in ice. Satan can neither walk nor speak; he is soulless but ravenous, a drooling monster with three conjoined heads, a dark mirror of the Trinity. The ultimate traitor who was cast out of heaven for his transgression, he is doomed to forever gnaw the heads of three other traitors—Brutus and Cassius (who betrayed and murdered Caesar) and Judas (who betrayed Christ). As he eats his eternal prey, Lucifer bats his wings, blowing a cold wind that freezes the center of the Earth, the bottom of Hell. Something less than a soul in torment, Lucifer is a negation; he is animated death.

IMAGINE

Your path has become even darker, narrower, more slippery. Crags of rock jut from the stone floor, tripping you as you walk. You squeeze between narrow passages that wind ever downward. The stones in your path become still larger, forcing you to clamber over, under, and around the jagged boulders. Your hands are scraped and bloody, your muscles ache, and despite the cooling air, sweat drips down your forehead, stinging your eyes. Finally, just when you think you are too tired to go any farther, you come out into another opening in the stone.

You have reached the cave's deepest level. The air is damp here, and you hear the steady drip-drip of water on rock. A footfall echoes against the stone walls, but you can see no one. Goosebumps run along your arms, and you shudder. Who knows who—or what—is lurking here in this dark space.

No fire lights this space, and you have to feel your way forward through the darkness. Something moves; you can feel the faint wind caused by its passing, but you see nothing, only shadows. There is nothing in the darkness to orient you, but you force yourself to step deeper into the cavern. "Who's there?" you call, your voice shaking.

You receive no answer, but somehow you recognize the dark presence that lurks here. It's your own shadow. It's been here all along, waiting for you.

Whatever shape it takes, however it manifests, the shadow represents the twisted truths we believe to be reality. It is our worst self. Our False Self. Like all shadows, it is only real so long as it avoids the direct light.

Just as Dante's Lucifer is trapped in ice, our shadow keeps us in stasis, weighed down, unable to escape. It drains us of soulfulness and vitality. It is that part of us that is trapped in the middle of our own inner hell, the part of ourselves of which we're most ashamed.

In the same way that Lucifer continually flaps his enormous wings, though he is unable to fly, the shadow's patterns are both repetitious and ineffectual. The same fears give rise to the same old strategies for protection. The ego feels threatened when it's denied what it craves, so it inflates itself with its sense of its own power—and yet it's unable to accomplish anything useful. In fact, often the ego's actions are destructive, both to ourselves and to others.

When I talk about the shadow, I'm speaking of the selfish aspect of ourselves that we keep hidden out of view, denying its existence even to ourselves.[1] It's the part of each of us that just wants its own needs met—and doesn't really care how that will affect others. And when those needs aren't met? The shadow sends surging into our consciousness anger, violence, lust, and all the other negative emotions that lead to suffering and dysfunction. And because the shadow is hidden, unconscious, we believe our emotions and actions are justified, rational. "They deserved that," we tell ourselves, "after what they did. It's only fair. I'm just standing up for my rights." Or our ego offers up some other rationalization for the shadow's dark impulses.

The shadow is our original sin. Our inherent vice. It pushes us to cheat, to use and exploit others. It gives rise to lust—and broken promises. It's the source of the deep-seated hatred and anger we harbor for those different from us. The human shadow leads to human trafficking, war, and the pollution of our planet.

While we may recognize the destruction and injustice wrought in the world by the ravenous human ego, we cannot distance ourselves from the darkness, for our own personal shadows contribute to the world's pain. Furthermore, the shadow's effects are also intimate and ordinary: when we explode in anger at our child, our shadow has taken control; if we feel a need to show off our luxury car or constantly pepper our conversation with our accomplishments, it's our shadow talking; our never-ending judgment of others comes from our shadow, and it's at the root of the falsehoods we tell to make ourselves seem more loveable. The shadow shows up in our abrasiveness and impatience, in our fiercest desires. It's the deepest part of the False Self, the source of fear and cruelty, injustice and manipulation.

The journey to the bottom of the cave means a direct, unmediated encounter with this dark and fearsome shape. Each of us have built contrived identities—our ego personas—which we use to ward off our most essential fears as well as the ugliest pieces of our hearts. Now, here at the cave's deepest and darkest level, we are being asked to sit squarely with these aspects of ourselves, with our brokenness and the ways in which we perpetuate brokenness in the world. To move toward wholeness, we have to confront that aspect within ourselves.

IMAGINE

As your eyes adjust to the darkness of this space, you can make out more clearly the shape of the presence that stands before you. Despite your fear, you sit down on the stone floor. You allow yourself to be open to this creature you have so long avoided.

The cold and damp from the stone beneath you seep into your body as you listen to the shadow's whispers. It knows your best-kept secrets, the most cutting insults, the shame and guilt and fear you have kept buried for so long. As you listen, you begin to recognize the shadow's many voices: friends, lovers, family, old enemies. Their voices grow louder, shrill and harsh and grating as they speak the vilest insults. A parent, a spouse, a child, a friend from your elementary school, a peer from your teenage years, all join in a terrible chorus of rejection: "I never loved you." "I wish you'd never been born." "You're worthless." "You're stupid." "You're ugly." "Everything you've ever done was for nothing."

Your ego screams at you to leave. "Run!" it cries. "Find something else to do. Don't read any more of that book! Don't stay here!" But you take a deep breath and force yourself to remain in this space. Nothing is required of you right now except listening to the shadow's many voices—and then, as painful images from your past flicker across the stone walls, you bear witness to scenes from your past. Perhaps you see someone from your childhood spit on you and you hear the cruel laughter of other children. A teacher embarrasses you in front of the class. A moment of violent abuse makes you flinch, but still you continue to watch and listen; a lover chooses someone else, a parent leaves you or rejects you, you betray a friend, your spouse cheats, you fail at your job. Images of dying loved ones join the panorama, and you feel the pangs of grief. Other images shove themselves forward, shouting, their faces distorted, enraged, disappointed, condemning. Angry. Threatening. Accusing.

You can barely breathe for the air is thick with malice. You want to run, but you know if you go backward, you will end up back where you started—and this monstrosity will still be here, lurking in the darkness far beneath the surface of your life. You consider standing up to fight the thing; perhaps if you are strong enough, determined enough, disciplined enough, you can destroy the shadow . . . but then you realize that fighting it only keeps you tied to it, defined by it. Your very hatred of it gives it energy. In fact, the shadow feeds off of the dualism that's created when you try to overcome it by sheer willpower.

Continue to sit here at the bottom of the cavern for as long as you need to do so; there is no rush, no timetable, no deadline you must meet. Allow the images and voices to swirl around you, while you neither fight nor flee. Let the fear wash over you like an immense tidal wave. Don't struggle against it. Instead, sit attentive, alert, aware. Allow yourself to feel whatever comes; when it passes, you will still be here. For now, simply welcome it, quietly, the way you would a guest in your home. Be present with it; sit with it; listen to it. Recognize it and name it. And as you do so, slowly you will begin to realize the pain, the fear, the violence are no longer real. They are the past, not the present. Their voices will grow more distant, and the images begin to fade.

A faint gleam filters between a crack in the stones, and by its dim light you can now see more clearly the stone walls that enclose you. The shadow moves past the light, blocking it for a moment, but then it flits back into the gloom. You squint through the darkness and make out skeletons strewn on the ground around you, their bones pale in the small shaft of light. Not everyone moves successfully through this space, you realize.

You look away, and your eyes fall now on rusty metal cages that lean along the cavern wall. A warped and leaning gate blocks the only way out of the cave (unless you were to turn around and retrace your steps). And so you continue to sit in this ancient prison with no clear path forward. Remember, there is no task you need to achieve here, no agenda to meet. You simply need to be here, for as long as it takes for you to begin to see through the shadows and phantoms your mind has created. Slowly, a new awareness grows. . . .

"One does not become enlightened by imagining figures of light," wrote Carl Jung, "but by making the darkness conscious." To experience the inner death and resurrection hinted at by the myths, spiritual texts, and the great mystics requires a confrontation with that which lies beyond the shadow, the very core of our False Self. This is what the myths indicate, and this is what we experience here in the cave.

Spiritual masters from many faith traditions, as well as Christ himself, teach that to truly live, we have to die before we die. To confront the dark heart of the ego is to face death itself, death of the body, of the mind, of meaning, of relationship. The death of what we want to cling to most, of anything from which we draw comfort and identity. Our patterns for survival. Our illusory projects for happiness. Our ego identities. Many of us would even prefer *physical* death to dying to the approval, affection, stability, or power we so deeply crave. We might also prefer physical death to facing the losses we've experienced.

The pattern of confrontation with a death-figure as the means of ultimate transformation is the same in all the great stories, including modern movies and stories. In Tolkien's *Lord of the Rings*, beyond the hero Frodo's battle with his shadow Gollum lies the death-figure Sauron and the specter of being consumed by the fire in Mount Doom. In Lucas's *Star Wars*, beyond the hero Luke's fight with his shadow Darth Vader lies the death-figure of the Emperor, and the specter of being consumed by the exploding Death Star. In *The Matrix*, beyond the hero Neo's fight with his nemesis Agent Smith lies the death-figure of the machine world and the specter of being destroyed there. In the Harry Potter stories, the shadow and death figures are combined in the villain Lord Voldemort, and the stories are constructed to suggest that killing him means Harry will die as well.

The ancient myths also contain this encounter with death. The singer Orpheus has to convince Hades, the god of the underworld, to let him return to the surface world with his beloved Eurydice. Theseus, hero of Athens, has to confront the monstrous Minotaur at the heart of the labyrinth where Athenian youth are sent as a sacrifice. Persephone is held captive in the underworld, until Demeter, her mother, can work out a compromise with death and darkness. The lesson from the world's great myths, including Dante's tale of his journey through Hell, is that we need to accept the reality of physical death as a natural part of the human experience, while also embracing the transformative process of the *spiritual death*, the death of the false ego structures we've built.

Notice that death is itself a captive in these stories, similar to the way in which Dante depicts Satan as a static figure. This is exactly what our shadow side causes within us: stasis, confinement, an inability to grow and mature. In a sense, we are dead inside; we are trapped, unable to truly live. And yet paradoxically, we fear the annihilation of this dead thing inside us. That fear hangs over this encounter with our shadow side, driving us to erect more false structures to protect ourselves. Our fear of death is in direct proportion to our illusion that we need our false identities to exist.

One of our deepest fears is that to give up our ego's programs for happiness, to give up what the False Self seeks, is to give in to death. At the most basic level, we fear death because we believe we *are* this body, we *are* these thoughts, we *are* these emotions. In fact, we have all these things, and we need to be good stewards of them, but over-identifying with them keeps us caught in the False Self. It takes a death—a true death, in the healthiest sense of that word—to free us from that illusion and open us to the deeper sea of grace, both for ourselves and for others.

In the previous chapter we touched on the three core needs or ego centers in the human experience, as articulated by Trappist Abbot Thomas Keating. These deep and unconsciously felt needs form the basis of the False Self as it manifests in our lives: the need for *safety and security*, for *affection and esteem*, and for *power and control*. These are the three inner needs underlying our sense of emptiness and craving, our fears and illusions. They give rise to the False Self's "programs for happiness."

These pursuits are our compensation for unmet needs during critical stages of development, which our minds have stored at a deep emotional level. As Keating puts it, the programs for happiness are based on:

> Our unconscious, prerational emotional programming from childhood and our overidentification with a specific group are the sources from which

our False Self—our injured compensatory sense of who we are—gradually emerges and stabilizes. The influence of the False Self then extends into every aspect and activity of our lives, either consciously or unconsciously.[2]

The ego can be thought of as a gnarled tree with a wound at its root. This original wound profoundly shapes our individual relationship to the outside world, how we perceive the world, and what we expect. The pain we experienced during a critical point in development—whether it was something as simple as a mother's business trip during a time in our childhood when we felt particularly vulnerable, for example, or more serious forms of neglect—forms the core wound. This gives rise to a core fear and a core need, which could be expressed something like this: "The world is inherently unstable, so I have to do whatever I can to fight against that threat, to make it secure and stable." This becomes an organizing principle for the developing ego. Personality traits, unconscious likes and dislikes, even friendships and community memberships can develop out of this deep core need.

Since our core needs will never truly be met from outside ourselves, we invariably become disappointed to one degree or another, and all our external pursuits become what Keating calls "programs for human misery." We like to think that proper education, assent to a value system, or even a conversion experience eliminates this False Self. We seek a shortcut, so that we need not face the dark creature in the buried cave. But there are no shortcuts on the inner journey.

In the Christian tradition, we are said to become "new creatures," and indeed, we may experience great newfound freedom through entering into a community and adopting a new set of values. Joining an expression of faith can move us out of destructive egocentrism into community-oriented living. When this takes place during particularly difficult times in our lives, it can expand us and give us new strength. But it is still an intermediate state of awareness. All too often, we confuse the beginning of the process of transformation with the end. And we can misinterpret spiritual experiences as evidence of lasting inner transformation. At its best, however, becoming part of an expression of faith only provides a context within which to uncover the unconscious motivations of the shadow.

In my case, I was raised in the church, having "given my life to Christ" at the age of four, been baptized at five, and spent my entire childhood, adolescence, and adulthood listening to thousands of sermons, singing thousands upon thousands of worship songs, participating in church plants and leadership, prayer groups and worship teams, retreats and Holy Spirit revivals, and finally, pastoral training—but my core issue remained unaddressed for many years. I had times when I felt closer to God or further away, but always this subjective emotion seemed a matter of my relative effort to practice moral virtue, read the Bible, or attend Christian functions.

Since the earliest age I can remember, I had a powerful need for affection and approval in general, and from females in particular. I developed an elaborate inner fantasy life to address this need and protect myself from the anxiety it triggered. Given the general strictness surrounding morality in my household and church communities, however, my inner desires had to be hidden at all costs. If found out, I knew I could lose the affection and approval I was getting from family. (Or so my emotional logic went.)

While we tend to designate puberty as roughly the age of sexual awakening and beginning of strong desire for the opposite sex, I was sexualized from the earliest age I remember. In any given social situation, I would identify the girl or woman most likely to give me approval and affection under the right conditions and mentally fixate on her, whether or not there was any interaction between us. When I was five, a babysitter was the target of those emotions; after my brother suggested our older male teenage cousin might "like" her, I was so overcome with jealousy that I clawed at my brother's face the way drug addicts might claw at someone trying to steal their drugs.

Romantic relationships continued to define me as I grew older. I had suicidal thoughts when my seventh-grade girlfriend told me she'd slept with an eighteen-year-old and was in love with him. I had already fixated on her as the solution to my internal emotional needs, and her confession seemed like the worst possible loss. In high school, when another girlfriend admitted she'd slept with someone I knew, the suicidal thoughts were even stronger.

At times, I felt guilty about my obsession with the opposite sex and the associated acting-out behaviors, but I had no deeper understanding of what was going on within me. Later, in college and seminary, I was still under the thrall of this one form of approval, this one validation of existence. I spent a great deal of energy trying to fight or suppress or numb this neediness.

Trying to be *saved* by a connection with a member of the opposite sex, I failed at relationship after relationship. Wounded again and again, I was unable to let go of my fixation on the very thing that was hurting me. I would pray and confess and feel remorse for various behaviors, and I'd go through periods when I felt I'd conquered this emotional habit—or that Christ had conquered it for me—now that I was attending chapel or reading my Bible. There was a certain smugness to this feeling, an ugly tinge of self-righteousness; I felt others were inferior to me if they couldn't achieve the same kind of spiritual control I claimed to have, the same kind of abstinence. But of course it was never long before I'd fall back into the same pattern myself. Then I'd experience the shame and guilt all over again.

I tried to understand where this hole inside me came from. Was it because as a newborn I was sent home from the hospital with a surrogate mother when my mom had postpartum kidney stones? Did the surrogate neglect me? Or was it caused by being the youngest in the family and feeling the need to have my masculinity validated? Cobbling together my story never changed the need or the behavior, nor did it change the shame and guilt.

Sometimes the problem seemed like something that was wholly immune to being healed by faith, much as Christianity can't make us no longer need air, water, or food. My pastors said I had a Christ-shaped hole in my heart, and yet the problem wasn't being addressed by participation in Christian community. There was a need in me so deep, so vast, it couldn't possibly be met by songs, sermons, prayers, and Bible passages. My actions and attitudes seemed to me to be in direct defiance of God's will, and I feared they would eventually land me in hell. Not until much later in my life, in twelve-step groups, did I experience the honesty, reflection, courage, and transformation that I'd found lacking in explicitly Christian communities.

For years, I was caught in a cycle of guilt. Eventually, if our energy is sapped again and again by an ever-present sense of shame and guilt, even that comes to be suppressed. I was overwhelmed by this enormous tangled bundle of emotions: the need for a woman's approval, the behavior, the fight against the behavior, the guilt over not winning the fight, and finally, the rejection of the guilt that inevitably ensued. I pushed the entire mess downward, hiding it from my consciousness, and in the process, my sense of vitality drained out of me.

This is what we do to ourselves. We bounce from wound-based need, to acting out, to guilt, to confession and temporary relief... then back to the need and all the way around again. Then we either distract ourselves or we condemn ourselves as lost causes. At the same time, in the midst of our own struggle and despair, we nonetheless apply the same logic to others, convinced if they were truly following Christ, they wouldn't be smoking or pregnant or skipping church or wearing black and listening to death metal or depressed or addicted to drugs. As we apply the condemning moral logic to others that we apply to ourselves, we are not only our own morality police, but we also become the morality police of others. In the process, we close off our capacity for giving or receiving transformational love.

There is another path. It's the path we take when we follow Dante down into the cave, where we fully confront our shadow and the death that holds it captive. Then, as we seek to grow in awareness, we make room for understanding; our vision becomes clearer, and we are able to recognize more quickly these thoughts, emotions, and impulses as they arise. Within the contemplative space, we no longer identify the thoughts that arise with our deepest self. We may always have our incessant thoughts, our fears, our impulses—but they don't have to have us. Over time, we can cultivate a spacious awareness that will give ourselves a choice of how to respond when these feelings arise.

Many people, including prominent church leaders, have failed to find this path. Disgraced pastors—men like Jimmy Swaggart, Jim Bakker, Ted Haggard, and thousands more—suffered great public humiliation because they never worked through their core conflict surrounding affection and approval. They were feeders and funders of the morality-police mentality, embracing a spirituality of perfection, working with great fervor and dedication—and then they were caught in adultery with a church member or with drugs or prostitutes. Nor are women immune to such ego trappings and the hypocrisy they engender. Aimee Semple McPherson, the founder of the Foursquare Church, the tradition in which I was raised, was a charismatic healer, preacher, and early twentieth-century celebrity who is rumored to have had numerous clandestine "flings."

When we hear about people like this, we often feel the temptation to self-righteously condemn them and their hypocrisy; we may even gloat over their downfall and savor the sweet irony. These were spiritual leaders who took advantage of the people in their congregation; they were wolves in sheep's clothing, hypocrites, adulterers, scum—and we take a certain pleasure in retributive justice. We like seeing the sinners on display in the public square. It's a juicy story for the tabloids, but it also consolidates our values and feeds our sense of smug superiority. (With the Pharisee in the Gospel, we say, "Thank God I'm not like *them*."[3]) This too is the ego at work.

Love, on the other hand, tells us to *see through* the behavior and understand its source. As the mystics teach, each of these people, like all of us, are shards of God, pieces of the Divine. But this Divine essence at the very heart of our consciousness gets clouded by the grime of ego, illusion, attachment, desire. We fall victim to our own unconscious processes, our unseen attachments, our projects for happiness.

Often, people who experience a "fall from grace" and the shame of exile from the great houses of the ego they've built, recall this fall (once the dust has settled) as the beginning of truth and self-awareness and freedom in their lives, painful as the experience is. Without their *felix culpa* (happy fault),[4] they could never have dropped their False Selves and begun to live the truth.

Rather than hissing the villain out of the community, we should applaud the arrival of this awareness and self-acceptance. God's good news is always about redemption and inclusion, about wholeness rather than guilt or condemnation. As Richard Rohr often writes, we usually don't get to God by doing everything right but by doing it wrong. It's when things fall apart that we become unmasked, forced to confront our true selves, and only then can we begin to make our lives and personas more deeply coherent with the truth. Moving toward this wholeness requires first *seeing* the reality, and then *letting go* of the habitual patterns of fear and desire that emerge from our wounds.

If your core ego need is *affection and esteem*, as mine is, you'll tend to fixate on approval from others. On a personal level, you want people to notice you, like you, need you. On a social level, this can inspire you in positive ways, since you'll likely have a passion for social justice. You want the world to be a loving, caring, compassionate place; heartlessness, callousness, selfishness, and exploitation make you angry. You yearn for restorative justice, and you like to hear stories of grace and mercy, or perseverance in the face of great suffering.

While this core wound can inspire you in healthy, constructive ways, it can also make you tend to focus on the world's victimizers: the heartless industrialist, the military-industrial complex, the racist, the sexist, and any other group or individual you perceive as being unjust. Though this tendency starts with the best of intentions, it can become its own kind of blindness, reading injustice into situations where it may not exist or exaggerating it where it does exist, sowing more confusion and discord rather than solving the core problem. Instead of actively working to build wholeness, you may unconsciously look for oppressive situations that offend you. On the extremely unhealthy level, people with this core need might even feel justified in killing those they perceive as oppressing the freedom of others.

People with this core need tend to live in places or take jobs where they can be of most help (where they can feel needed). Meanwhile, the core fear associated with this type is that the world is inherently vicious, cold, uncaring, and unjust. Both tendencies arise from the core wound of a felt rejection or neglect, often in childhood.

If, on the other hand, your core need is for *safety and stability*, you value a sense of order. The family system that is most comfortable for you is one that is firmly structured (and possibly patriarchal). You might experience anxiety if your environment gets too messy or disorganized, and you crave a clear moral order. You believe in a very precisely defined right and wrong, and the concepts of *discipline* and *character* resonate for you. These can be strengths that help you to excel at various life tasks.

At the social level, you are likely to want retributive justice for crime, while spiritually, you are more prone to believe in a literal hell for sinners in the afterlife (or at least some spiritual system of retributive justice). In the political arena, you may fear instability and be susceptible to leaders that prey on that core fear, since it triggers such a visceral response in you. Because you believe that order is necessary to the safety and well-being of society, you see nothing wrong with institutions that have a rigid structure that enforces what you think of as moral behavior.

People with this core need tend to believe in meritocracy; in other words, people get what they earn. Seeing the world through this lens can keep you blind to systemic injustice, since you may believe people largely get the material comforts or treatment they've earned through their own choices and behaviors. At the extreme or unhealthy end of the spectrum, people with this core need, unmitigated by conscience or restraint, may be willing to kill to bring about the order they believe is necessary. People who allow this core need to run unchecked may be Fascists, Nazis, or belong to some other group that is so convinced their version of reality is the correct one that human life is expendable in bringing it about.

Rather than finding ways to build wholeness in our world, if you have this core need you may unconsciously look for immoral behavior that offends you, and you may advocate for punishment for those who violate the moral order as you perceive it. When you start perceiving people or groups of people as obstacles to the order you wish to see—whether those people be immigrants or conservative politicians; rebellious teenagers or members of an unfair educational system; or believers in religious faith that could be Muslim, Christian, or something else altogether—you place them at a distance from yourself; you demonize them and fear them. They become abstractions only, rather than nuanced human beings like yourself. If you remain frozen in this state, you will never achieve spiritual maturity; you can organize the world, but you will never love it as it is, in all its messiness.

As a result, you won't be able to move on to the next plateau of inclusive love, but instead, you'll stay mired in oppositional thinking. Someone will always pose a threat to your core need, giving you yet another thing on which to fixate. The fear stays constant; only the object of the fear changes.

You'll tend to respect established institutions like churches, the military, and law enforcement, and you may prefer to live in suburbs or small towns where the kind of order you crave can be maintained most easily (and if you can't actually live someplace like that, you'll romanticize those places). The core fear giving rise to this desire is that the world is inherently dangerous, chaotic, and unstable with no discernible meaning, coherence, and order to it, unless we work diligently to bring it about. This fear festers out from the core wound of a childhood lack of stability and security.

Finally, the core need for *power and control* creates a worldview that focuses on the survival of the fittest.

Only the strong survive—and if you have this core need, you will do *whatever it takes to be strong, to "win."* You see the world as an amoral competition for scarce resources. Since there's not enough to go around, you want to be one of the people who get as much as you can of whatever it is you feel you need (whether that's money, power, prestige, or belongings). You enjoy competition (so long as you can win), and you may actively seek out challenges to overcome; your strengths are your self-discipline and willingness to undergo hardship in order to succeed.

This tendency will make you gravitate toward arenas that are inherently competitive, like professional sports, business, or politics. It may make you inclined to demonstrate your power over Nature with hunting trophies, or you might emphasize your job title or other indicator of status. Whatever your conquests are, you like to put them on display, and you get a thrill out of exerting control over others. Highly aware of power dynamics, you may work to develop ever more efficient ways of getting and maintaining power. You focus on clear status symbols, and you may gravitate toward urban communities, where social stratification is more obvious and your higher status will be more visible. If you don't have the individual gifts to obtain the kinds of power you deeply desire, you will associate as closely as possible with those who do.

Unfortunately, the satisfaction you piece together—whether through your own power or by identifying with a group in power—is always a fragile one. All power is in constant danger of being usurped, attacked, and subverted. This awareness can keep you enslaved, spurring you on like a master's whip to pursue your ego projects and shape the world according to your core need. In doing so, you participate in the cycle of sin and death, staying spiritually immature. Your concept of God may be limited to a Divine back-up for your ego project; in other words, you identify with an omnipotent God who triumphs over the world's "losers," and you cast the Deity in the role of supporting all your efforts to control others. When carried to extremes, this core need can drive people to kill those they feel are weak, those who hold them back in some way or who dare to compete with them.[5]

Since people with this core wound tend to be more overt and unapologetic about their ego pursuits, other ego types often demonize them. In doing so, we can miss the logs in our own eyes,[6] our own ego-driven misperceptions. We all have a set of cardinal sins on which we fixate, external behaviors we see in others of which we most certainly do not approve. These are things we can point to on the surface layer of our awareness that undermine the social and moral order *as we see it*.

Christ's definition of "sin," as given in the Gospels, was more comprehensive than that. For him, sin referred to the whole system, from the wound, to the fear, to the desire, to our external ego-driven projects. All of it—not just the external behaviors—constitutes a sin *system*. It's what he referred to in the Sermon on the Mount, when he said we're focused too much on the external act and not the internal self; we live according to dictates of the False Self and its ego projects. When Jesus spoke about cleaning the inside of the cup,[8] he was getting right down to the heart of the matter.

And what are we supposed to do about it? *Repent?* That's what the church tells us to do—but what is that, exactly? We often take repentance to mean a display of deep, genuine remorse. We think if we're truly sorry and genuinely apologize with a contrite heart, then we'll be forgiven, and that's what repentance is. Being forgiven, however, does not necessarily mean we are free of the sin system. We may still be stuck in the same ego cycle, and without deeper awareness, we will likely act out again sooner or later, even if it's in a more socially acceptable way.

We are trapped by our own egos and lack of consciousness. Our shadow side distorts our vision, handicaps us. We spend our spiritual energy fighting this inner demon rather than experiencing fullness, vitality, and a true sense of agency in our lives. This can remain true even if we appear outwardly virtuous and manage to suppress from view whatever energy comes from our shadow.

Being stuck can be far subtler than the obvious drug addiction or depression. In fact, people in those dysfunctional states are paradoxically closer to healing than many who present themselves as well-adjusted, because they're closer to what the twelve-step groups call rock bottom, which (as Dante also tells us) is the only beginning to the way back up.

Since each of the core ego needs sees the world dualistically rather than as an integrated whole, each is prone to fixating on its corresponding objects of fear. Whether we fear we will never get the love and affection we need to survive, we fear an ideological agenda will undermine the moral fabric of our family and country, or we fear someone younger (or prettier, smarter, more skilled, more powerful) will come along and take away the success for which we've fought so hard, we all experience some form of fear. Some of us are so deeply oriented by fear, we don't even notice it anymore.

If our lives or communities are oriented by fear on *any level*, we still have the inner work to do of confronting its source if we're going to enter into spiritual maturity. We have to die to this False Self. The

Christian scripture addresses this directly, claiming that "perfect love casts out fear,"[9] but the way of love, the way of maturity, must also be the way of death on some level. To reference a more modern mythic story, think of the scene in the final Harry Potter book where Harry gives himself up to die for his friends—and then discovers that it was only the part of the evil Voldemort hidden within him that had to die. We too must experience something similar if we are to live lives that are controlled by love rather than fear.

If we seek only justice and comfort in a community with strong moral values, we will remain asleep, unaware of both our shadows and our True Selves. Meanwhile, to a greater or lesser extent, our shadows maintain their influence. On the other hand, sometimes we've fought this battle so long and hard we can fall into cynicism or despair, and then we assume that anyone who claims spiritual maturity and insight must be a fake or a fraud. As a result, instead of identifying with a community, we isolate ourselves.

But there is a Middle Way. This is the way of Christ, the mythical way, the mystical way. Instead of fighting the shadow, we have to identify with it, to acknowledge that this, too, is who we are. When we turn from our ego projects, we lose our need to blame others. We can stand face-to-face with our ugliest self, with our dark twin, our devil, and acknowledge that this is a part of us. We take responsibility for our shadow, without blame or guilt or sentimentality, without projecting it onto someone else—and as a result, the monstrosity begins to lose its power. As its defenses crumble, we can clearly see the wounds that fed it. This awareness frees us from being held miserably in its thrall.

We have to cultivate our spiritual state of receptivity and openness to allow this change to take place.[10] Deep attention to this process is called spiritual practice. In my own case it was a combination of rock-bottom experiences of addiction, of acting out, being caught, standing at a point of no return that brought me to a crossroads where I finally recognized the essential energies that dominated my life. This time I made no dramatic promises to change myself; instead, I simply became committed to witness, to watch, to accept, and to fashion a space around the entire dynamic, a space formed by habitually entering in the silence of contemplative practices, allowing the destructive patterns to become more fully visible.

This process stripped me bare of my defense mechanisms; I stood naked and vulnerable, with no comfort in sight, but instead of scurrying quickly in search of somewhere to hide, I made a daily habit of simply resting in the presence of God, of consenting to Divine presence and action within. Into that spacious silence, a quiet peace began to take root, a simple joy, a capacity for delight. Not wanting, not judging, simply being, I began to experience the ways in which causeless, non-contingent joy is possible.

God—or the Universe, depending on the word you give to these concepts—may have the tools for our deep healing and lay them out for us, but at some point it is we who have to pick them up and get to work. We who must show up. We who must till the soil. Sometimes we have to diligently and carefully pull up weeds from their roots. When we deliberately unearth the pain we buried in the dirt, it loses its potency.

IMAGINE

Here in the bottom of the cave, the very air seems charged with fear—your thoughts, your cravings, your addictions, your attachments, your violent thoughts against those who have wronged you, your betrayals. The images that haunt you in quiet moments are all here, now amplified.

Then the dim light grows again in the distance. You walk toward it, but you find the rusty gate still barring your way. You try to climb over, but it is too high. You strain to push against it, to try to pull it open, but the ancient metal will not give way. You pry and kick and strain, sweat dripping from your face, but nothing works; the gate still bars you from going toward the light.

Finally, with a sense of defeat, you slump down onto the floor of the cave to catch your breath. The darkness is still full of images, haunting you. But then a quiet voice tells you, "Don't resist. Observe yourself having the thoughts, observe yourself having the emotion as if from a distance, as if it were someone else. These are the thoughts. These are the emotions. This is the reason these are coming up. Just observe and identify what you see. Don't fight them. Don't feel guilty about them or afraid of them. Simply accept each thing you see."

Slowly, you allow yourself to relax into the space. You let the images play out in your head, and you neither fight nor flee, neither rage nor rail; you simply accept. You accept the humiliation of your past actions. You accept the pain, the sense of loss and betrayal, the shame. You permit each feeling to come . . . you welcome it into the space and observe it with curiosity but without judgment . . . and then you allow it to pass on. Anger, spite, resentment, fear, disappointment, hurt, hatred; each take their turn. You notice each feeling, and then you let it pass.

In this dark space, you simply sit and breathe, and finally, when you are ready, you shift your attention to your own breath. The shadow and its power over your inner state wanes. You realize you have been sitting with your biggest mistakes, your deepest pain, your ongoing struggles—whatever they are—and you have survived. The space where you are sitting seems to open up a little, because large enough to contain your own story. You look at it with a loving gaze, and you feel as though a curse has been lifted from you. Although you are still in the dark, a sense of possibility and agency open up within you. It's a state of grace.

The narrow finger of light from outside the cave catches the white bones in the opposite corner of the cave. Emboldened now, at peace, you get to your feet and take a step toward the pile of skeletons. To your surprise, light seems to emerge from between a rib cage. As you draw closer, you see something behind the bones, on a small ledge in the rock face, something that gleams intermittently when the dim light catches it.

You reach in between the bones, making some of them clatter to the ground, and grasp this small shiny object, pull it out, hold it toward the dim light. It's a key.

You rush to the gate and slide the key into the lock. The rusty metal scrapes and gives way as you turn the key, and you push the gate open just enough to squeeze through. And now you can see the light is the mouth of the cave. It's the way out.

As you move upward, you experience a growing sense of levity. Tired, dirty, but with a hard-won peace, you slowly make your way toward the light.

Walking through the cave, we confronted suffering in the world, suffering in the family, and suffering in ourselves. We sought a deeper awareness of our thoughts, behaviors, and the internal processes that give rise to them. This allowed us to articulate our core wound, one of the key sources of our inhibitions and destructive patterns. With this awareness, we can let fall our core fears and ego projects, we can go about what the Bible calls metanoia, or turning and transcending. We are no longer tethered to the way of the flesh, so to speak, but can now go about the work of the spirit. Through this process of acknowledging our False Self and identifying its patterns we begin the process of allowing our wound to be transformed. This operation of genuine transformation and healing ripples outward, touching the lives of others and bringing that grace and healing into the world.

But a moment of awareness in and of itself will not bring about lasting change. If we make this mistake, we will swing back and forth between addiction and awareness like a pendulum. There is more work needed. Now we must climb up. Having confronted our inmost self, we can grow, expand, and mature. We are no longer bound by self, by ego projects, trapped by our own fears and desires; now we can move outward. The mystics teach that when we reach a high degree of awareness and turn from our ego projects, love can work through us. Before we were limited in this capacity. We now have to exercise those muscles, to learn that language. This climb is about learning to become manifestations of love in the world. It will take diligence, community, and a growing awareness of our lingering patterns, which have been laid bare but not yet dissolved. It is we who have to continue to till the soil.

WAYPOST 4 EXERCISES

Select **at least two or three** exercises:

1. **Core Need:** What is your core need or ego center—power and control, safety and security, or affection and esteem? What desires and fears are associated with it? What behavior patterns emerge from it? Remember, this is not something hard and fast but rather something that often changes in different contexts and circumstances. Over the course of your life, however, you will likely be able to identify

a center of gravity, a common pattern of relationships, causes, and addictions that tie back to one
core need.

2. **Timeline:** Plot a graph including five-year incre-
ments along the x-axis (or horizontal plane). Draw a
timeline of your own life up to now, identifying the
highs and lows as you experienced them. Are there
recurring patterns as to what constitutes the highs
and the lows?

3. **Manifestation:** How has this ego center affected
your behavior in relationships, in the workplace,
and in the interests you've pursued?

4. **Audio Divina:** Listen to a song that invokes for you
the confrontation with the shadow or False Self. (My
selections: "Digging in the Dirt" by Peter Gabriel,
"Moonshiner" by Bob Dylan, "State of Love and
Trust" by Pearl Jam.) Write about the way in which
the song connects to your reflections.

5. **Visio Divina:** Watch the video of Johnny Cash's
cover of Nine Inch Nails's "Hurt" (you can find it
online). Write a reflection on the video.

6. **Poetica Divina:** Read the poem "Psalm for the Lost" by Paul Mariani (you can find it online). What resonates with you most from the poem?

7. **Lectio Divina:** Romans 8:1–12 (Read, Reflect, Respond, *Rest*).

NOTES

1. This is a bit different from the Jungian definition. Jung defined the shadow as our hidden or unconscious aspects, *both good and bad*, which the ego has either repressed or never recognized. He wrote, "Confrontation with the shadow produces at first a . . . standstill that hampers moral decisions and makes convictions ineffective or even impossible. Everything becomes doubtful" (*The Collected Works of C. J. Jung*, "The Conjunction," Princeton University Press, 2000, par. 708). But he also wrote, "The shadow is merely somewhat inferior, primitive, unadapted, and awkward; not wholly bad. It even contains childish or primitive qualities which would in a way vitalize and embellish human existence, but—convention forbids! (ibid., "Psychology and Religion," par. 134). In other words, Jung believed that the shadow is not only the dark underside of the personality. It also consists of instincts, abilities, and positive moral qualities that we have kept buried (perhaps because for some reason they were deemed unacceptable in our family of origin or community). As you confront your shadow, you may want to consider whether this dark creature also holds strengths that, if you brought them into consciousness, could enrich your life.

2. Keating, Thomas. *Invitation to Love: The Way of Christian Contemplation*. (Rockport, MA: Element, 1992), page 3.

3. Luke 18:11.

4. The Latin expression *felix culpa* derives from the writings of Saint Augustine regarding the Fall as the source of original sin: "For God judged it better to bring good out of evil than not to permit any evil to exist." The medieval theologian Thomas Aquinas referred to this line from Augustine when he explained the principle that "God allows evils to happen in order to bring a greater good therefrom" and indicated the relationship between original sin and the Incarnation. In the fourteenth century, John Wycliffe stated that "it was a fortunate sin that Adam sinned and his descendants; therefore as a result of this the world was made better." John Milton wrote in *Paradise Lost*: "O goodness infinite, Goodness immense! That all this good of evil shall produce, And evil turn to good; more wonderful Than that which creation first brought forth Light out of Darkness!" This paradoxical perspective applies to the microcosms of our lives, as well as the macrocosm of the Fall and Incarnation.

5. Daniel Plainview of Paul Thomas Anderson's 2007 movie *There Will Be Blood* is a recent example of this archetype.

6. "And why worry about a speck in your friend's eye when you have a log in your own?" (Luke 6:41, NLT).

7. Matthew 5–7.

8. Matthew 23:26.

9. 1 John 4:18.

10. *Cultivate* is a word rooted in the same Latin word that *culture* and *cult* are. The original meaning of *cult* was "an act of worship or reverence," and all three of these words grew from the root word *cultura*, which had to do with preparing the earth for crops, with the additional meanings of honoring, tending, caring for, respecting, and guarding. The Latin word's many shades of meanings interweave our relationship with the Earth, our relationship with each other (our "culture"), and our relationship with the Divine.

Where woundedness can be refined into beauty a wonderful transfiguration takes place.

-JOHN O'DONOHUE

Our real journey in life is interior; it is a matter of growth, deepening, and of an ever greater surrender to the creative act of love and grace in our hearts.

-THOMAS MERTON

PART TWO

THE
OUTWARD
WAY

The psyche can find completion and coherence only when it lives within, or has living within itself, a complete and coherent image of the universe. The great reconciliation of the Bible with classical learning entered popular consciousness through the mediation of artists like Dante and the architects of the great cathedrals, who imagined a whole world story with mind, heart, and flesh.

–MARTHA HEYNEMAN

The cathedral is an instrument of religious action. The space of the cathedral can be compared to the void before creation, when all is still potential. This is the mother's womb into which the Logos descends, and from which all creation derives. Like Dante's great poem, the cathedral can enact transformation.

–DOUG THORPE

Into the Cathedral

Waypost 5

Once Dante takes the full measure of Lucifer and understands his frozen, static state, the anti-love that freezes the center of Hell from his mechanically beating wings, Dante moves through to the other side. Following Virgil through the hole at the bottom of Hell, Dante scales down Lucifer's giant hairy torso. When he finally emerges on the other side, he's standing at the bottom of a crater and sees Lucifer's legs sticking up out of the ground. Dante is confused and disoriented. Everything is upside down!

Virgil helps him understand. They've climbed through the center of the Earth, and now they're in the Southern Hemisphere, on the other side of the world, where everything is inverted. The crater where they stand was created when Lucifer was cast down from heaven. As they climb out of the crater, Dante breathes in the clear, cool air; he looks up to see the stars on the eastern horizon shining like oriental sapphire.

The wanderers now encounter Cato, a principled, virtuous soldier and statesman who had committed suicide rather than compromise his values. He now guards the way to Ante-Purgatory, the area before the climb up the mountain begins, and he tells the travelers that before they meet the custodian angel whose keys unlock the gate up the mountain pass, they'll need to wash off from Dante's face the stain and grime acquired in the journey through Hell. To climb this path, he needs to be cleansed.

We, too, seek this kind of cleansing.

IMAGINE

Continue now on your own journey up out of the cave toward home. See the light up ahead. Draw closer to it. Feel the hard rock underfoot give way to softer ground. You breathe in the smell of damp earth and granite. Ahead, you now see an opening in the rock face, with patches of green around the opening. You emerge from the cave into a cool breeze, fresh air, dawn, a thin light growing on the eastern horizon.

As you leave the cave behind, you see in the distance a hill with a path leading up and veering out of sight in the distance. You walk along the path, grateful for the open air, feeling a new lightness now that you have left behind your ancient wound. In spite of the long climb, you experience an influx of energy and vitality. After a short while, you see, off to the right, across a field with scattered trees, a country abbey made of ancient gray stones with carved wooden doors. Graven saints in miniature peer down from alcoves. A monk stands near the doorway with a bird on his shoulder.

The day brightens as the dim light of the dawn gives way to morning. Tired, thirsty, in need of rest, you walk up to the door and open it. Leaving behind the cold and dark, your fears and wounds, your shadow, you enter into the sacred space. You find there a small group of monks chanting; melody and harmony converge and rise like incense, like prayer. One novice silently offers you a flask of water. You take. You drink. As you hand the flask back, the novice shakes his head; with a gesture of his hand, he invites you to keep it.

With a sigh, you sink down onto one of the wooden benches. Light spills through the jeweled images of sacred myths recounted on the stained glass windows high on the walls. You are here to receive, to rest—and to find a new direction.

In traveling the downward path into the suffering of the world, the suffering in our families, and the suffering within ourselves, we developed a better understanding and an increased awareness of the mechanisms of our False Self, the systems whereby we engage in destructive patterns and our own ego projects. By confronting our shadow and the threat of death that stands behind it, we allow a clearer vision of ourselves to emerge and a new way of relating to the world to develop. We make way for our True Self. This next process of discovery is the Outward Way, which brings our newfound balance out into the world.

But before we begin that journey, we, like Dante, need to cleanse the grime of toil and effort from our heart. We recognized our core need, our ego mechanism, and our attachments. We let them fall. We *turned* from them. Seeing them clearly for what they are is like seeing behind the magician's tricks. We are no longer in thrall, no longer living out of illusion. We may have residual thought patterns and mental habits, but now we know where they come from and we can begin to slough them off like old skin. This is the cleansing that Cato knew Dante needed.

Then, once we've dropped our old habits and patterns, the worn-out organizing principles of the constructed self, we need a new direction to find our way home. We need to get *reoriented*. This will not happen automatically, without some effort and intention on our part.

I experienced this sense of reorientation when I arrived in southern California to attend seminary. Up until this point, I had been torn in several different directions, toward friends and family on another continent, toward a fading romantic relationship in another city, toward personal ambition, toward dealing with my own fears about direction, vocation, and competence, toward a desire for a life of faith and deep questions about that life as I understood it at the time.

The cities of Pasadena and close-by Los Angeles were bustling, noisy, congested places, focused on youth, wealth, glamor, power, and image. The seminary campus was a circle of quiet within that noise. In the corner of campus was a small prayer corner, dimly lit, covered with wood and ivy and decorated with plaques displaying Bible verses, with a few benches available to sit and pray. I found myself drawn to this place of stillness and refuge, and I went there often, taking short daily breaks from the constant internal and external noise. In such spaces of stillness and separation, we not only find rest, but insight, direction, perspective. For a short time, I was able to suspend the pressures and uncertainties of my life and emerge reoriented.

We do not travel Dante's road only once; life sends us along it again and again. Each time, the road may lead us deeper and deeper, asking more and more from us. In my own life, after I had graduated and had been teaching for a few years in the inner city, I reached a point where I again needed to be reoriented, but this time on a far larger scale.

I felt I had let several conflicting dreams simply dissolve. My wife and I had determined that entering into a PhD program in literature wasn't an economically viable option for me. In choosing to marry and settle down in America, I had distanced myself from friendships and trips back to Europe, where I had felt a greater sense of purpose, identity, and vitality. I had gone through the mourning process of several deaths, of lives unlived, of old friends lost, of family members long deceased, of a musical career, of an academic career. Now, I had little left in the way of focus, vitality, and purpose. I was burned out and felt deep disorientation, disappointment, and resentment. The bitter voice in my mind became a broken record of resistance to the situation in which I found myself. Day after day, I asked myself, "How did I end up here? Failing at marriage with the wrong job in the wrong town in the wrong *life?*"

None of these aspects of my life helped support my own unconsciously held ego project: the deep need for affection and esteem. As a result, I continued to build up a daily inner resistance to my life situation. Over time, even my body began to break down. Within three years, I had three surgeries. The near-constant desire to escape felt like a lead ball in my gut. This was a daily rejection, a daily death. "This isn't what I signed up for," I kept saying to myself.

I started drinking more during the work week, which meant I woke up tired and even angrier with my life. I was engaged in a vehement inner resistance against my life situation, a psychological and emotional contraction that led directly to my own physical breakdown. I thought of people who had fallen into depression, alcoholism, or suicide; "So this is how it happens," I said to myself. I was badly in need of inner work, but also of rest, direction, reorientation.

One symbol of reorientation that has provided a place of rest and transcendence for spiritual seekers down through the centuries is the cathedral. To enter a cathedral is, in a sense, to enter a womb. Think of Notre Dame—our Lady, our Mother. This is a space meant for our formation, for our growth, for our nourishment. We understand we are not fully formed; we are a perpetual work in progress. Cupping hands to receive communion is an act of receptivity, a grace. In so doing, we recognize our vulnerability, our interdependence; we affirm the possibility of grace, of community.

Read in a certain light, Homer's *Odyssey* is about right cultivation, and we can apply this lesson to our inner space as well. In the epic poem, bread and wine are symbols of a civilized people, evidence of cultivation. The lawless, according to Homer, live in wild, overgrown lands, while the civilized cultivate and transform the land. They till the soil, they sow, they harvest, they grind wheat into flour, they turn the flour to bread. Wine, too, is a product of refinement and cultivation, of effort, of discipline, of *work*. The energies of sun and earth and water combine with the work of hands.

In the ritual of communion, we receive bread and wine, partaking in the rhythms of harvest and vintage, of Nature transformed, of a greater order beyond our individual selves. We affirm that we are part of a process of transformation. In the Christian tradition, this transformation is identified with the person of Christ; it is the process of grace. Having undergone transformation, we in turn become agents of transformation ourselves, fully aware that while we are not its source, we can choose to align ourselves with it.

This grace can come to us in the form of a timely conversation with a friend, a book or song that speaks to us, a moment in Nature—anything that nudges us toward some new opening. In my case, a friend who had spent a month as a guest at a monastery gave me a prayer bench, a simple construction: three small wooden boards to help me kneel a little more comfortably during prayer. To have a device like this spurred me to set aside time for prayer in the morning. I decided to get up a little earlier, light a candle, read through the Psalms, just a couple each morning. Then a new acquaintance mentioned he led a weekly Centering Prayer group and offered to share some of his material with me. I had practiced this form of prayer, but only in fits and starts, and now I became almost painfully aware of the difference it could make. An inner slackening began, a loosening of my nonstop, futile push-back against the walls of reality. New possibilities emerged. New awareness. New directions. I became reoriented.

For the medieval mind, to enter a cathedral was to become *oriented*. This word, in its most ancient form, originally meant "to rise like the sun." All properly built cathedrals were constructed to face east, toward the sunrise. To enter the cathedral, to face east, is to become *oriented*. Theologically, this corresponds to the Son's rise, to the new life of the Resurrection. The symbolism of death and resurrection is at work in the cathedral's very architecture and in its relationship to the surrounding geography. Within a cathedral, we become situated, grounded, set in proper relationship to the world.

Another way in which the cathedral orients us is through the story on the walls. The stained-glass windows depict elements of the biblical story. During the medieval era, people were mostly illiterate, and only those educated in Latin could read the Bible, so its events were recounted on the windows in simple pictures for the layperson. The sunlight shining through the windows is another metaphor for the story of Divine grace at work in the world. We become profoundly aware that it is by this light we know the story, by this light we are able to see.

This can also become a powerful image of the self made whole. We will always have experiences of brokenness, but what if our fragments were reassembled in coherent order? What if we were part of a greater whole? What if, even after being stained and broken, we were cleansed and then put back together and flooded with light? What if the light reflected and refracted and took on new coherence and meaning through *us*?

There is another sense in which the cathedral is sacred space. For the medieval mind, the physical, material world was a representation of the spiritual world. Given this sacramental imagination, the cathedral was intended as a grand symbol, manifesting the qualities of the Divine, a redeemed creation made visible. For medieval architects of the cathedral, the pillars, arches, and shafts of light were meant to imitate the natural illumination in a forest, but with an additional sense of symmetry, order, and proportion. Remember Dante waking up in the forest at the beginning of *The Divine Comedy*, lost, exiled, and disoriented. The cathedral in a sense represents the redemption of our fallen nature; it is also a space *within which* it can be redeemed.

The understanding of a sacramental imagination is foundational for artists and theologians. Part of the work of the sacramental artist is to reveal *Logos*: the pattern, rhythm, balance, harmony, and order that underlies all of existence. This is also the work of sacred architecture in space, using the principles of physics and geometry. Like the Eastern mandala, the cathedral was intended to be a picture of the cosmos itself. This Greek term—*kosmos*—originally meant order or harmonious arrangement. It provides a sense of the scale of the sacramental imagination that gives rise to the cathedral. The one precedes the other.

A similar sense of the Divine-made-manifest applies to the other sacred arts in their appeal to our senses. From this perspective, that which manifests the qualities of beauty, balance, and harmony, that which speaks to the spirit, that which elevates our being, also communicates the Divine.[1] Across the various disciplines, artists talk about the kind of surrender that can take place either in the act of creation or in the act of experiencing certain kinds of art.

Classical writers consciously also constructed their works in a way similar to the principles that underlay a cathedral's architecture. Homer's *Odyssey* was originally part of an oral tradition and sung by the bard on a succession of nights in a strict meter;[2] the rhythm and repetition had an incantatory quality for the listeners, bringing about a spellbinding atmosphere in which they could visualize the events narrated in song. Similarly, Dante's *The Divine Comedy* was written in a strict form called *terza rima*.[3] It is this underlying order that provides order, harmony, and balance to the work, and it is within this underlying framework that the sound and sense of the language play out. In both cases, this order and balance was intended to reflect or manifest the Divine. Homer invoked the Muse to "sing through him" at the beginning of the poem, so that he may become a vessel of Divine communication, while Dante, who wanted to manifest the Divine truth of the Trinity in his disciplined poetic structure, was closer still to the intention and sacramental imagination of the architects of the Gothic cathedral.

The other arts can also express a similar sense of the sacred. We speak of the *grace* of a dancer. We speak of being *transported* by a painting, a poem, a piece of music. Musicians and athletes describe moments of self-transcendence, of alignment with some deeper order as an experience of being in "flow" or in "the zone."⁴ All of us, whether or not we are artists or athletes, experience moments of this kind of synchronicity or beauty in our ordinary lives. We may lack the language to speak of it or the framework to make sense of it, but we sense we've experienced something sacred, something larger than ourselves in which we were privileged to participate. We have a sense of both channeling within us something majestic and being caught up in it.

The structure, pattern, and rhythms at work in sacramental architecture also connect with the monastic tradition. Dating back to the early Church fathers and codified in roughly 500 CE as the Rule of St. Benedict, monastic life involves removing oneself from ordinary pursuits of society to live a life of discipline and prayer. This involves daily rhythms, which vary according to monastic tradition. For medieval adherents to the Rule of St. Benedict, the daily prayer consisted of readings, chants, singing of Psalms, and reciting of prayers during the eight canonical hours, beginning with *Matins* at midnight, *Lauds* at 3 a.m., *Prime* at 6 a.m., *Terce* at 9 a.m.,

Sext at noon, *None* at 3 p.m., *Vespers* at 6 p.m., and *Compline* at 9 p.m. Each office involved its own rituals, with the time between set aside for specific tasks. Although this tradition has changed and adapted in different contexts, the core principle of living a life of discipline to participate in a Divine rhythm and an underlying order have stayed with us. We are not all called to the monastic life, obviously, but reorientation means that daily life itself can be turned into a poem pointing toward the sacred.

My own reorientation emerged from my engagement in contemplative practices. I began to let my daily experiences, frustrations, and resentments play out against the backdrop of a larger rhythm of which I was just a small part. I became more attuned to my own mental patterns, able to notice what caused my stress level to spike and my inner resistance to kick in throughout the day. My morning routine became an indispensable part of my day, allowing me to stay in touch with an underlying peace, even in the midst of daily tension. I was learning a rhythm of rest.

As we follow Dante's road, we've entered now a space of restoration and healing, of Divine rest here in the cathedral. This is a Sabbath time, a time to withdraw from the noise of ordinary life. The ancient Hebrew concept of Sabbath was not a passive kind of rest; rather, it was a time of remembering, of staying rooted in communal identity.

One difficult element of modern life is the way in which our sense of identity is tugged about, pulled apart, fragmented. For the ancient Hebrews, remembering the collective story of Exodus and gathering in worship helped organize life and identity. Mirroring the account of creation when YHWH rests on the seventh day, the Sabbath is also a time of reflection, of looking back over the week and examining our choices, our relationships, our work, our direction, our internal state. We look backward in time to move forward in maturity and awareness, to grow.

The Greek language has two different words for time. The first is *chronos*, which gives us the words "chronology" and "chronicle." This term refers to sequential time, the cycle of Nature, of seasons, of cause and effect, of work, of social station, of the process of physical birth, aging, decay, and death. *Chronos* is our default, everyday time. The other word for time is *kairos*, or sacred time. *Kairos* is, in a sense, beyond time, at least as we know it. *Kairos* is the timeless, the supreme moment, the eternal *now* in which we connect with the transcendent. Within *kairos*, we also can get in touch with our deepest self. As we follow Dante, this entire mythical journey in a sense takes place in that sacred time—a time of healing, of reorientation in a space apart from the everyday.

The experience of the timeless, this penetration through the veil of *chronos* into *kairos*, is a nexus, a focal point. At this point in the journey, we pause to remember and take stock. We look backward toward the past, to the stories of our mythical tradition, in order to move toward wholeness of being, to experience transformation, to internalize the lessons. We reflect on what we have seen in the cave. What do we take away? How will we stay rooted in our True Self—the moment-to-moment loving awareness beyond the ego's striving? We cling to community for strength; we cling to core principles to navigate the difficulties to come, whether internal or external to ourselves. *Kairos* is the space to reflect on those relationships and values, to reflect on our interdependence with them, and to make a habit of gratitude.

As I made Centering Prayer, Psalter, and Lectio Divina part of my daily routine, these practices became a window to *kairos*, a small penetration of the veil of reality into the timeless. The daily discipline made an opening in the incessant clamor of thought, concern, worry, and insecurity and allowed a momentary illumination, a transcendent perspective to enter. The memory of that light could then become a mental touchstone for me throughout the day as stressors and pressure mounted. My morning routine became for me a daily point of *orientation*.

Of course, there is also a danger in our lives of grasping too desperately at spaces of rest and reflection, especially if we have experienced a tremendous amount of pain or suffered a profound loss. As much as we appreciate hospitality and healing, of respite, if we cling to them too desperately, they can become traps rather than sanctuaries, providing comfort but not growth, a tranquilized lull but not wholeness. Along the same lines, Anthony de Mello speaks of the occasional conflict between his role as a psychologist and that of spiritual director. Those in therapy often want to feel better and ask for a technique to make that happen; they don't necessarily want a wholesale change in the way they look at the world or to confront the pain in their lives at a core level and move through it.[5] They want relief from pain rather than the astringency of healing. The goal of our spiritual journey, however, is wholesale change. This always involves risk, because by definition change brings losses (as well as gains)—and the specter of loss generates fear and anxiety.

But not here, not now, not in *kairos*. Here we get to detach from these concerns. Here we can be filled up; we can receive, rest, and simply *be*. But we still need to get *home*. We must not forget the journey we are on.

In Homer's epic poem of the mythical journey home, *The Odyssey*, the temptation to forget the journey takes several forms. First is the island of the Lotus-Eaters, where those who partake of the lotus become forgetful of their homeward way. The most direct parallel in our modern experience, of course, is substance abuse, but we have many other forms of addiction that help us forget our journey and keep us waylaid.

In another passage of Homer's poem, the danger comes in the form of the Sirens who sing of Odysseus's exploits in Troy. Their songs about his honor and accomplishments pull him toward the past. Sailors who hear the songs and move closer crash on the rocks and perish. Odysseus is able to survive not through force of will but by plugging his men's ears with wax and having them tie him to the mast (because he wants to still hear the song!). Unlike the Lotus-Eaters episode, this passage does not represent slipping into numbness and forgetfulness but instead points to an unhealthy focus on our own achievements, staying mired in the illusion of past accomplishments and the comfort that can bring to our ego when faced with uncertainty. The Sirens speak to the danger that can lurk in the act of remembering, of reflecting—not on reality as it is or on our core purpose but on our False Self, our ego and its little projects to ward off anxiety and pain. In accepting this false reality, we run the risk of stagnation; our vision blurs, and we become limited in our ability to experience healing ourselves or to help bring it about for anyone else.

IMAGINE

For now, here in the cathedral, you lay all fears to rest. Tomorrow will bring other troubles, but in this temple, this place of *kairos*, you pierce through temporary concerns and glimpse a deeper order. You participate in that order, partake of it.

You may not be home yet, but you've been given a sanctuary. Even though you know you have to move on, for now, simply rest in a moment of awareness. Give yourself permission to breathe in this sacred place, knowing that tomorrow, even in moments of suffering, you can draw from this timeless space when you sense the underlying order, the Divine rhythm beyond your little ego.

A novice approaches you in silence and guides you away from the sanctuary to a small, bare room. Bread and wine are arranged on a simple table. He motions for you to take, eat, and then points with an open hand toward a bed with clean linen. He turns and takes his leave. The door creaks shut behind him, leaving you alone in this small, safe, quiet place. Take a breath. Relax. Let yourself rest.

WAYPOST 5 EXERCISES

Select **at least two** exercises:

1. **The Cathedral:** Find a cathedral in your area. Most are open for prayer during the day. Make a visit. As you enter, pay attention to the use of architecture, order, balance, symmetry. What strikes you most about the place? What is the experience of being there? Does it affect your inner state? Are you moved into the silence or do you resist it? Do you choose to sit and pray or do you walk around and take in the space through the senses?

2. **Flow:** Write down three experiences in your life of beauty, transcendence, synchronicity, or flow: occasions when you had a sense of a deeper order. Maybe for you this was rock climbing or painting or playing the piano or playing tennis—some moment of deep focus and a temporary loss of self-consciousness.

3. **Sacred Relationship:** What relationships in your life provide a sense of communion or make possible a greater giving over of yourself to another person? These could be old friendships or connections with children or partners. Describe the quality and experience of those relationships as best you can or describe a time when you felt most held by this relationship.

4. **Audio Divina:** Listen to a song that invokes sacred rest for you. (My recommendations: "O Lord in Thee Is All My Trust" by Jan Garbarek and Hilliard Ensemble, or "What a Day" by Greg Laswell.)

5. **Sacred Activity:** List five activities that deeply relax you. Commit to doing one this week. Maybe it's going to a movie, doing yoga, calling an old friend on the phone (or better yet, going to see that person), or getting a massage. Pay attention to the change in your thoughts and emotions. Then write about your experience.

6. **Lectio Divina:** Matthew 11:25–30 (Read, Reflect, Respond, *Rest*).

NOTES

1. St. Thomas Aquinas writes of the characteristics of beauty: integrity, harmony, and *claritas* (brightness, vividness).

2. For the curious: the meter was dactylic hexameter, or six feet of the LONG-short-short syllabic pattern, like the English word MUS-ic-al.

3. A three-line rhyme scheme in which the last word of line 2 of a given tercet becomes the last word of line 1 of the following tercet, making the rhyme scheme aba bcb cdc, and so on.

4. Mihaly Csikszentmihalyi. *Flow: The Psychology of Optimal Experience* (New York: Harper & Row, 1990).

5. Anthony De Mello. *The Spiritual Wisdom of Anthony de Mello* (Altenmunster, Germany: Jazzybee Verlag, 2012).

Creative work is play. It is free speculation using the materials of one's chosen form.

–STEPHEN NACHMANOVITCH

The job of the artist is always to deepen the mystery.

–FRANCIS BACON

Preparing for Reentry

Waypost 6

Climbing up the terraces of Mount Purgatory, Dante eventually comes to a brilliant white marble wall on the mountain face, where he sees stories engraved with stunning realism. Portrayed on the wall, the angel Gabriel appears to Mary, the obedient girl bent low to the heavenly messenger; King David dances half-naked before the ark; the Emperor Trajan stoops down to promise justice and mercy to an old widow whose son has been killed, delaying his military campaign to tend to this local matter. Each of the scenes depicts acts of humility in the service of others. Mary humbles herself before the angel; King David humbles himself before God and God's people; the Emperor Trajan postpones the grand designs of empire to tend to the needs of a someone of lowly status.

Turning from the engraving, Dante sees hunched figures moving toward him with giant stones on their backs. These merchants, generals, and artists, Virgil informs him, were prideful and arrogant in life, and so now are they bent low here in Purgatory, slumped beneath the weight of their penitence. The former arrogance of these individuals is in sharp contrast to the stories of humility engraved in the white marble.

As Dante moves through this terrace, he learns the right use of his creative energies and talents as a poet and artist, which is to neither create spectacle nor fuel his pride but rather to tap into deeper truths and reflect them to others, to both teach and learn the virtue of humility, the practice of right seeing, of alignment and right relationship. He expands his sense of vocation to include not only the work he does, but how he goes about that work and its greater purpose.

As he moves to leave the first terrace, an angel guarding the path brushes its wing against Dante's forehead, erasing one of the seven Ps (standing for the Latin *peccatum*—sin or wound) that was etched into his forehead at the beginning of his climb. Having learned this stage's lesson—that his creativity must be put in the service of a higher truth, that his greater part to play is the embodiment of humility—his sin is removed, and he finds his burden lightened as he walks on.

IMAGINE

You rouse yourself from the restful quiet of your room in the abbey. Light is gleaming now through the single window; a new day has dawned.

Rested, feeling lighter, you leave the room. The novice is waiting, and with a warm smile and deep bow, he silently hands you a filled water skin. You thank him with a simple bow of your own, open the heavy wooden door, and leave this sanctuary.

The morning air is fresh against your face as you step out onto the road. Behind you, monks are already going about their morning work, sweeping the courtyard and cleaning the space. Close by, farmhands call to oxen as they set their hands to the plow, singing beneath the light-filled sky.

As you set on your way, your feet brush against wild grass that grows along the edges of the path. Leaves whisper in the breeze overhead. After the confinement of the cave, with its damp and dark, you enjoy the sense of openness. The way is smooth underfoot, a relief after the bruising rocks within the cave.

After several miles, you see a distant bridge, with a town further on beyond it, but the trail leads you into a forest, blocking your view of what lies ahead. As the open sky and scudding clouds give way to patterns of light through foliage, you feel compelled to stop for a moment. You take in the scent of soil and dead leaves, the sound of birds and foragers in the undergrowth, the shafts of light falling through the trees.

Sit, lean back against a tree, and breathe in. Notice the new perspective lower to the ground. From this position, you see things you normally pass by, preoccupied with other concerns, and after a few moments, you become conscious of the patterns of Nature at work here. Ants form a line up a tree and go about seeking food for their colony. A breeze flutters the leaves, and you see a caterpillar making his way across a leaf. In the soil beside you, a worm tills the earth. All around, you see the evidence of Nature's work being done. There's a pattern, an intricate order at work. Transformation is going on everywhere you look.

Part of our journey home, in fact the overall purpose of pilgrimage, is the process of self-discovery, while at the same time situating ourselves in the world as part of an order that transcends our small self. One key component of this process is restoring a sense of the sacred. In our desacralized world, this usually means experiencing a radical shift in our way of seeing, a change in perspective.

Dante's lesson was that the prideful want to set themselves apart from the cosmic order, exalt themselves above others, seeing the world around them as a means to pursue their own selfish ends, as something to be controlled. They are fundamentally self-centered. The virtue of humility, by contrast, is rooted in underlying wisdom. It recognizes the greater order in which we live and move and have our being. It is aware that each of us is one small thread in the great weft of the world. In a state of alignment with the principles and energies that animate life, that give fullness and vitality, we facilitate the greater wholeness; we become channels of *shalom*; we play our role in forming cosmos from chaos. As agents of selfishness, however, we obstruct that movement. Part of our journey home is to attend deeply to these patterns of life in the world, in others, in ourselves.

Humility is not self-effacement but acceptance and participation in the greater rhythms of *being*. This involves both labor and creativity, work and play, giving and receiving. It requires skillful responses to the energies around us and a wisdom born of humility. During this part of our journey, we want to rediscover this pattern, to sit and receive, to *perceive*, to truly see.

In my own life, I've been involved in obvious creative endeavors, like publishing poetry, recording albums, and writing books, but I've also engaged in more laborious tasks, like planning and delivering lessons, attending drawn-out company meetings, managing classrooms, grading, running departments, planning organizational infrastructure, drawing up communication plans for organizations, developing online course launches, and so on. To be effective in any of these endeavors draws from a creative source and then channels it, remaining attentive, present, and alive to the dynamics in play. Yes, there's the necessary task of mastering a discipline, whatever our field, but it's just as important to interface with a larger source of inspiration to bring quality, energy, and resourcefulness to that discipline. One way we stay connected to that creative source and a way we can restore a sense of the sacred, is through rediscovering a sense of play.

My first conscious experience in my own life of an opening in the doors of creativity happened in a writing class. The setting was a conservative Christian college, where the general campus discussion circled around establishing and policing rigid moral boundaries, primarily concerned with asking, "How far is too far?" This question was applied to dating and sexuality, but also to product consumption, video games, food, language, dancing, everything. Truth was abstract and predefined, usually by authority figures. In this context, the writing professor's simple invitation to *tell your truth* had a profound impact on me.

As I began to explore with language the subtle textures of sense perception, of feeling and memory, of experience and longing, I felt liberated. My awareness, both internally and externally, expanded beyond a preoccupation with narrow moral categories and anxieties about conformity. The professor asked us to attend to the way people interact dynamically with their surroundings, their desires, motivations, and frustrations, without judging first and foremost. Truth became a process of discovery and experience.

Freed from having to force my experience into a prepackaged evangelical mold, I felt as if I'd been given permission to take off the blinders, to see beyond a very narrow, confined, predetermined space. I could take delight in things for their own sake, not for their relative value to evangelism and without a sense of either procrastination or indulgence. There was nothing to control, nothing to fear; all I had to do was notice and take in.

What a liberating invitation: "Tell *your* truth." I began by playing with my trove of gathered memories, emotions, impressions, *experienced* truths on the ground floor of my mental house. I described what is. But then the invitation drew me in even deeper: Describe a dream you had that affected you strongly. Turn it into a poem. Write a story about something that happened to you as a child, but from someone else's perspective. Write a story from the perspective of an object you've owned. The professor challenged us to take our internal experiences out of their boxes and to play with them. Experience and imagination had validity and beauty, in and of themselves, and not only when condensed into a tidy morality play or a formulaic narrative form of Christian testimony. Folly, anger, confusion, desire, the entire human experience, no part left out or swept under the rug.

As Dante learned, true creativity has nothing to with self-indulgence and prideful spectacle in the name of self-expression, which can lead to egocentric art interested only in shock value. And although artistic achievements can and do inspire a deep moral vision, creativity's serious playfulness must come first in the mind of the artist. Otherwise, if the primary purpose is to convey a heavy-handed message, the work will sink beneath the weight. It will become propaganda, not art. Artistic transformative truth comes from a deeper source than the kind of surface legalism and fear-based conformism evident in many religious contexts. Art that is both powerful and humble emerges from genuine experience, not from prescription.

In my writing class, I was taught how to participate in *right seeing*, without the constant implied pressure to be a representative of moral certitude, which confines consciousness and distorts our perception. Certitude is stifling, leading to superficiality and pretense, to the denial of the shadow, to inauthenticity. Hearing my profession's invitation to tell my truth instead allowed me to take a step back and simply observe, before applying labels and moral categories. It gave me room to recognize and honor experience as it is, not only as it ought to be.

Later, when I graduated from college and arrived at seminary, I was mourning a relationship and in constant financial straits. During the first quarter, I mostly stayed confined to my apartment, leaving only for classes and then coming back to read, research, write, and fix meals. Physical, financial, and social circumstances confined and constrained me. I lost the sense of playful creativity I had learned in my college writing class.

Then, during the second quarter of the school year, I joined the Arts Concerns Committee and, along with a small group of classmates, began going through Julia Cameron's *The Artist's Way*, a book designed to help people get unstuck creatively. With exercises to help get me out of my head, to point me toward the energies at work all around us, I started shifting into a different mode: I became curious, receptive, involved. I gathered leaves and read up on local trees and plant life. I took pictures of local landmarks in Pasadena: the Colorado Street Bridge, the Laemmle Theater, Vroman's Bookstore, Cal Tech, the Arboretum, art on the seminary campus, City Hall, the city fountains.

The act of seeing inspired fresh avenues for writing. I wrote poems. I became curious about new writers. I was more attentive to the life going on around me, rather than narrowly focused on the limitations I had come up against in my personal life. And I was suddenly over-flowing with inspiration: I wanted to learn guitar, start a band, write a screenplay, publish poems. Where before I saw only obstacles or possible failure, I could now sense possibility, a desire to try new things. I felt connected to a greater pattern, a greater order.

None of the actual work I produced during that time had lasting merit or warranted publication; none of it was "good," in that sense of the word. That would come later, but the creativity wasn't wasted; it cultivated an inner space and freshness that became a lasting bench-mark for the life I wanted to live. The excitement of that period was an initiation into the processes of inspiration and discovery, reflection and creation.

The challenge—I later found as I was busy with teaching, administrative work, business—was to stay aligned and attuned to this state of vitality and curiosity, so that I could tap into and channel something "far more deeply interfused."[1] I've learned that I can access that energy through reading; through playing with language, as well as with sounds and songwriting; through listening closely to music; through exploring and traveling, through journaling and writing; and through contemplative practices. Other folks tap into it through sports, hiking, mountain climbing, walking their dog, painting, gardening, making furniture, organizing a wardrobe, snowboarding, playing a trombone, dancing, cooking, designing a room, building computers, building a business, or building a home. The consistent thread in all these things is that this energy is *generative*; through it, something new comes into the world, however transient it might be.

In her fascinating study *The Breathing Cathedral*, poet Martha Heyneman suggests that part of the power of art and poetry is their ability to situate us inside patterns of meaning through the senses, through the body itself.[2] In music, in dance, even in sports, we have a sense—some sort of internal image—of the whole piece, the whole pattern, whether that's in a piece of music or the parameters of play, and we also understand where we are at any given time in space and in time relative to the whole. We enter a *cosmos*. This consists of an unfolding pattern, but it also suggests that this pattern is unfolding *toward a particular purpose*. As poet Robert Bly puts it, "If you memorize any work, you bring it into the body. And then you are participating in space. And then it can become sacred space."[3] This kind of experience provides an inner ordering, a harmonization, and potentially an experience of transcendence.

Heyneman suggests that this kind of sacred art had its apex in the late medieval period, in works such as *The Divine Comedy*, Chartres Cathedral, and Aquinas's *Summa Theologica*. In this premodern period, before scientific rationalism became the order of the day with a worldview hollowed out of meaning, people still felt themselves part of a Divinely organized cosmos, in which their daily experience, even gravity itself, partook of a greater sacred order that had its beginning and ending in God. The impact of poetry—here understood to be not just patterned language but that which embodies a truth beyond the merely rational—arises in part from its power to restore that sense of existing within a cosmology, an ordered pattern which includes an awareness of the sacred, and in which we can orient ourselves. To read *The Divine Comedy*, with its symmetries, its unwinding *terza rima* form, its movement toward God, and its understanding at any given moment of where the pilgrim (and the reader) is on that journey home, is to allow ourselves to be held within a sacred order.

The ancient myths also point toward a deeper design at work in the living world in which we participate. Theologian Andre LaCocque suggests that the Hebrew creation myth sets up a dynamic interplay between order and disorder.[4] Permanent order is not a fait accompli at the moment of creation, but a process within which we are situated as human agents. Goodness, home, Eden, and Kingdom are built when we align ourselves with the Divine laws inherent in the created order. For LaCocque, this underlying pattern, this Divine law, is what Eastern traditions call the *Tao*; it's called *Wisdom* in the Hebrew Proverbs; medieval mystics portrayed this central organizing principle as *Sophia*; and it's the Eastern Orthodox principle of the *Logos*.

The dynamic order in disorder is what makes possible the material world, as well as wisdom, virtue, and the experience of beauty. It's the energy underlying geometric patterns that give rise to all living forms. It's in the double helix spiral of our DNA and in the spiral of a galaxy. The New Testament writers experienced this Divine quality as uniquely and singularly manifest in Jesus of Nazareth, as the *Christ* and *Son of God*, the human embodiment of *Sophia*, the incarnate *Logos*. And in the same Gospel, *we, too*, are called children of God, capable of manifesting the Divine. With this understanding, we become the agents that make Divine patterns operational in the world; we are the human partners of God in shaping cosmos from chaos, order from disorder, *shalom* from violence.[5]

We experience this through the body, as well as the mind and spirit, and we have a foretaste of it in a well-ordered poem and in architecture where the craftspeople have paid attention to intricacies of form. We hear this deeper meaning in transcendent musical patterns. We taste it in healthy community, in loving relationship, in recognizing ourselves as an integral part of a larger whole. This *is* wholeness. Dwelling in this space is itself a kind of homecoming.

Our greater work is to open ourselves to the process of being transformed into wholeness and acting out of that wholeness in the world, facilitating the movement toward *shalom*,[6] toward a sacred balance as taught by the great spiritual texts. This kind of health, order, and proportion requires that we recognize our interrelatedness. We seek peace, justice, righteousness and love, which are all *relational* terms; they only exist *between* people.

When we have a sense of inherent joy in work, or we perceive something beautiful in Nature or in art, we usually have a sense of *right relationship*, of timing and movement, of symmetry of shape, of form and content in proper proportion, of a "just measure" in the music.[7] The best work, whether on a canvas, in the boardroom, or on the operating table, has an inner quality of rightness, an appropriate and skillful use of the materials available in the given situation.

We train our minds, our bodies, our hands to become conduits through which this quality can manifest in the world, allowing it to be brought about in and through us. Through our work in the world we return to right relationship. Since we exist within nested systems— economic, social, political, environmental—both the work we do and our approach to that work influences the greater web. And all this is both the way home and *home* itself.

Scholars suggest that Homer's Odysseus finds his way home through the Greek quality of *metis*—wisdom and craft. To exhibit metis is to be attentive and alert to the reality of the present moment, the opportunity for *kairos* to emerge into *chronos*. Odysseus shows *metis* in his ability to craft stories, to use persuasive speech off the cuff in difficult situations. So does his wife Penelope in her nightly weaving and unweaving that keeps her ravenous suitors at bay. *Metis* creates cosmos out of chaos.

But chaos, too, has its place in Homer's story. Not simply evil, chaos is a propulsive, dynamic, generative energy. Poseidon, god of the sea and earthquakes, personifies the primordial energies in *The Odyssey*. His power can be destructive, tearing ships apart and bearing Odysseus to distant lands—or it can carry Odysseus home. The difference lies in how Odysseus meets this primal energy. Resistance, self-assertion, and pride lead him adrift on the open sea. Craft, cunning, skill, wisdom—*metis*—guide him home.

I'm suggesting that in order for us to manifest this quality, to be alive and alert to the requirements of the moment, to manifest wisdom and skill as we follow our journey, we have to lay down the False Self, its noise, its cravings, and be truly present. We have to learn humility, not just as a value we espouse but as a quality of being we embody. In Homer's poem, the blind seer Tiresias instructs Odysseus to deny himself before he can find home. Then, once Odysseus finally reaches Ithaca and his beloved Penelope, the symbol of reunion in the story is the marriage bed, crafted from an olive tree still planted in the ground, an image that points toward the skill and wisdom, including the virtue of humility, that bring Odysseus and Penelope together again. In the same way, these qualities realign us; they restore right relationship to the land itself, which becomes the very foundation for the family, central to the health and wholeness of the entire community.

As I struggled to become a successful teacher in the inner city classroom, I needed to learn *metis* as it applied to the classroom. I had to attend deeply to internal and external rhythms. To be equal to the challenge of thirty-five teenagers confined to a classroom for two hours at a stretch required learning the rhythms of the year; it meant accepting the anxiety, resistance, and acting out at the beginning. It also asked that I learn personal rhythms of adequate exercise and sleep; of meal timing and portions for energy throughout the day; of planning for the year, the month, the week; of managing assignments, grading, instruction, and student work. It was like learning to dance—so many things to keep track of all at the same time.

Early on, my overestimation of my own intelligence and abilities was an obstacle that hindered my ability to achieve *metis*. If the school system was failing, I reasoned, there must not be enough intelligent people truly dedicated to getting things done right. In my arrogance, I assumed I was intelligent and dedicated enough to do the job. Instead, I found myself drowning. I couldn't keep up with the pace, couldn't manage to get students motivated, interested, or performing. I couldn't even maintain positive relationships with some of the students and colleagues. Within six months, I realized that while I might write a decent college paper, I needed to hone about thirty other skills to be an effective teacher. I was far from the most dedicated, intelligent, energetic, and effective teacher on staff. A personal breakthrough came when I read research on the assessing teacher versus the visionary teacher.

The assessing teacher introduces subject matter and assesses the student's ability to master it. Teachers with this perspective think in terms of fixed ability; they have a fixed mindset. I realized this was how I had been teaching. The sheer volume of writing assignments was too overwhelming for in-depth grading, so instead, I was getting a feel early in a class for students' abilities and using that as a shorthand for assessing their future work. It's an easy trap to fall into, if only for self-preservation, but it's biased, deterministic, and limiting.

Visionary teachers, by contrast, understand where they want the class to go and communicate that clearly and skillfully. They have a growth mindset and use encouragement and correction to help students reach the goal. They don't limit their students by shutting them up inside mental boxes and categories.

Guess which one is more effective, the static or the fluid, the closed or the open?[8]

Coming out of the static box where I had put both myself and my students, I could see new possibility. I became interested in how students process information, and I changed instruction, assignments and communication style accordingly. I moved from pure self-preservation to facilitation for others. From static to dynamic teaching. In and through me, something new was becoming possible. I was starting to learn the dance.

Even with that shift, the demands of the job could be overwhelming. To stay present, to stay motivated, it was essential for me to connect to primordial energies, to return to aspects of play: to read a Dostoevsky novel, attend a poetry reading, play basketball, play with language.

At play, we are unself-conscious, disinterested in a particular outcome or recognition from others. We simply take joy and delight in the process itself, whatever it might be.

At play we are also willing to learn. We stay in a posture of humility, just as on your journey you sat on the forest floor beside the path, close to the earth. Etymologically, the word "humility" comes from *humus*—earth, the soil—suggesting lowliness and self-effacement, but also receptivity and fecundity. At play, we forget about our egos and open ourselves to new thoughts, new ideas. We both widen our gaze and sharpen our focus as we continue our homeward journey.

Play connects us to the elemental energy around us. Some people find this energy in direct contact with Nature, in which so many beings are at work in interconnected patterns of living relationship.

The sense in which I'm using the word *play* doesn't only refer to the outward and active, but also to the inner play of observing, connecting, imagining. This sort of mental play can mean watching the clouds and imagining the shapes they take. It could be looking at a tree and envisioning the forces that shaped it into its current form. So many things can be turned into a state of playful meditation, facilitating a sense of connection and inner alignment with a greater pattern and order. Wherever and however we enter into this mental state, it is a creative, generative force at work in our lives.

IMAGINE

Here on your journey, as you look around you in the forest, you realize that the monks back at the abbey, the farmhands working in the field, the ants and the caterpillar crawling along beside you, the trees, the soil, the sky, the light, are all interwoven in an ongoing process of change that is at the same time held by consistency, a framework within which this change takes place. You allow yourself to sit with this awareness, soaking it up.

In doing so, you feel both humbled and at the same time inspired with a sense of the world's potential and possibility.

An essential quality of Nature and of our own lives is change within form. The child becomes taller and stronger; the adult eventually becomes weaker and smaller; caterpillars turn into butterflies; acorns turn into saplings, which turn into trees, which one day fall into the ground and go back into the soil. These energies are the basis of ongoing creation, of ongoing life. Just as the natural world undergoes the continual transformation of change—the unfurling flower, the shifting ocean— we channel that same energy in the creative act. This capacity to navigate change within form, to skillfully respond to it, to stay present and adaptable through creative interaction and response, is truly the quality of *metis*, the Greek notion of Wisdom.

We need to stay open to the primordial vitality at work in the world. In his reflections on the relationship between humans and the environment, poet and essayist Gary Snyder suggests two ways to connect with this animating energy, this underlying life force he calls "the wild." The first is through immersion in wilderness and direct encounters with the wild in its different manifestations; this allows us to become more aware of the wild within ourselves, to connect with it on a more fundamental level, allowing for greater understanding of our kinship and place within the natural order. The second way to tap into this quality is through the act of creativity.[9]

Snyder himself connects with and responds to this energy through the discipline of poetry, a form of concentrating meaning through patterned language. Poetry has long been closely connected to the creative act. In Genesis, YHWH *speaks* the world into form out of *tehom*, the abyss, which is not nothingness, but a primal substance, a potential energy. Theologian Catherine Keller suggests we might better understand the Genesis creation story if we change the traditional understanding of creation *ex nihilo* or *out of nothing* to creation *ex profundis*, that is, creation *out of the deep*.[10] YHWH, too, shapes cosmos out of chaos.

The Anglo-Saxon term for poet is *scop* or maker, and our English word "poetry" comes from the Greek *poiesis*, to make, to give shape. Not only does scripture describe God as the primal Maker, Jesus, too, is portrayed in the act of making through poetry, both theologically, as one "through whom all things came into being," and literally, through his parables and storytelling. When modern scholars retranslated portions of the Gospels from Greek back into the Aramaic in which Jesus originally spoke, they identified several poetic devices in his language, including the use of four-beat rhythm, parallelism, alliteration, and assonance in several of his teachings.[11] These are the tools of a poet giving shape to meaning. In poetry, the truths of a deeper order are given voice, body, shape, and form through a particular kind of concentrated language—through dynamic energy concentrated within the discipline of form. This is the essence of the creative act. It underlies the kind of work we often find most rewarding.

Creativity involves both a posture of awareness, of sharp receptivity to experience, and the ability and perseverance to craft that experience into a form through refined skill. This takes time; it requires an acceptance and a joy in process. Eventually, though, a convergence occurs, as we grow in our discipline, when the work seems to take over and we forget ourselves. We enter into that state of balance between energy and form, what professionals in many fields call a state of *flow*, and we sense that we have become channels of a process that is larger than ourselves. As writer Madeleine L'Engle puts it, "When the work takes over, then the artist is able to get out of the way, not to interfere. When the work takes over, then the artist listens. But before he can listen, paradoxically, he must work."[12]

This flow state is close to what the Greeks called *anamnesis*, or *unforgetting*. The Zen masters described it as a state of no-self. Jesus called it becoming like a child. It involves being playful, curious, inspired, awestruck; it asks that we forget self and attune ourselves with a larger reality. While we are here, we move away from a need for vengeance, vindication, and validation.

Creativity is generative and generous. It does not hoard. It gives of itself. It moves through us like grace, to be passed on. This is the state that is brought about through self-emptying, through humility. Over and over in the Gospels, Jesus tell us that it is not the self-righteous who inherit the Kingdom, the Divine state of internal being, but the humble. Our full humanity is linked to our capacity for this kind of humility. Cultivating this space of humility helps us stay receptive, attuned, open, creative. It can help us move from resentment to communion.

In my own experience, there's a kind of magic when the constantly shifting realities of experience and emotion coalesce in the creative process, whether in prose or poetry, songwriting or photography, but also in the well-delivered lesson or company presentation. A moment occurs that's like midwifing something new into existence. This is the moment we move past imitation into some kind of genuine expression. It's when we *find our voice*. It's when our memories and ideas and conversation and experience are given shape, form, coherence and texture. It's cosmos out of chaos. Even when I create something I'm satisfied with, I'm also aware of the sheer volume of missteps it takes to get one song, one poem, one essay right. There's extensive work in just moving *toward* quality achievement. And the very best work inspires new work, triggers new emotions, thoughts, and creativity; suggests new paths and possibilities; and partakes of a greater whole.

First comes the act of inspiration, which means both Divine guidance and *to breathe in*. This is the first step in going about the work that is uniquely our own. In this way, tapping into a creative source can be a kind of infinite well that keeps giving of itself—but it does not happen passively; we have an active role to play, first, by consciously opening ourselves to experience, remaining alert and responsive, and then *doing* the work, bringing our skill to bear in the tangible world. This work can broaden our awareness and attentiveness. It can allow us to draw from the wild, dynamic, generative forces at work in Nature, as well as in ourselves. Through this, we may also find our place within the greater weave of the world—which can be both humbling and restorative, reminding us of our small part in a greater whole. At our best, we are channels and vessels of a greater, intuitive knowing that stretches far beyond an individual mind's capacity. Staying interconnected with this restorative energy allows us to contribute to the world, to pursue our vocation.

Alignment with the greater whole, attending to it physically, socially, spiritually, is part of our greater work. As we draw life and energy from a creative, generative source, we partake of the same wildness that animates the natural world around us. Attending to this process, to what brings about joy both for ourselves and others, brings us to a deeper understanding of our work in the world.

IMAGINE

Stand up from your comfortable spot on the forest floor. Take a moment longer to remain there in this quiet green space, sensing yourself connected with the energies at work here. You are a part of it. Your very breath binds you to your surroundings. You're dependent on the trees for oxygen, as they are dependent on your carbon dioxide, and you are both dependent on the water, the sun.

As you focus on the forces at work in Nature and the intricate processes that exist, you become more deeply attuned to these forces at work in yourself, the many interconnected systems of which you partake. A dynamic symphony is playing: the slow rhythm of the forest, the movement of the insects with their brief lives, the flight of birds, their songs, the movement of a deer, all of which forms a continuum that includes you as well: this intricate matrix of unfolding Being. You are part of a greater whole.

At this stage of the journey, you're not ready for any great creative work. To attempt anything like that would be premature. Instead, this is a phase in which to play, as a child does, taking time to explore the world and your relationship to it. It's a time to simply breathe.

Take as long as you need to linger in this awareness. Then, when you are ready, open yourself to the call of the ongoing journey. Feel the pull toward home. Take one last deep breath here in the forest, acknowledge the creatures, their lessons, their participation in the very wildness of which you, too, are a part.

You smile as you take in the beauty of this quiet living space—and then you turn toward your path again. You begin walking in the direction of the distant village you glimpsed beyond the forest.

WAYPOST 6 EXERCISES

Select **at least two** exercises:

1. **Creativity:** What is the most satisfying creative experience you've ever had? Why was it satisfying?

2. **The Dream:** How did you dream about your adult life when you were a child? Imagine a "day in the life" if you had achieved that dream. Give as much detail as possible. Let your imagination play.

3. **The Life Dream:** What changes would you make in your life if money and time were no object? Write down five things and flesh them out in some detail.

4. **Life-Giving Activity:** List twenty things you enjoy doing. Pick one and do it this week.

5. **Sacred Art:** What are your favorite pieces of art? List five. These can be paintings, music, sculptures, movies, anything. Why do you think these works in particular resonate with you? Are there common threads? Write down what they seem to have in common.

6. **Create:** Make something this week: create a collage, write a song, write a short poem, paint something, take some photographs. Don't know where to start? Pick an already-existing work you like and imitate it, using your own perspective and experience. There is no right or wrong way to do this!

7. **Observation:** In the wilderness or a natural setting, pick out a single tree or bush to observe. Spend five to ten minutes watching that single organism. What does it look like now? How might it look in other seasons? What history might it have? How might other organisms depend on it?

8. **The Meal:** Bake something or make a meal that takes longer than fifteen minutes to cook. As you work, pay attention to sound, color, smell, taste, and texture. How does the experiencing of feeding others feel to you? Write a journal entry about it. What did you make? For whom? How did they respond? Describe the experience.

9. **Audio Divina:** Listen to a song that invokes for you a sense of sacred or redeemed creativity or play. (My selections: "Clam, Crab, Cockle, Cowrie" by Joanna Newsom and "Olana" by Marc Cohn.)

10. **Lectio Divina:** Exodus 36:1–7 (Read, Reflect, Respond, *Rest*).

NOTES

1. The phrase comes from William Wordsworth's poem, "Tintern Abbey." Here's the entire passage: "I have felt / A presence that disturbs me with the joy / Of elevated thoughts; a sense sublime / Of something far more deeply interfused, / Whose dwelling is the light of setting suns, / And the round ocean and the living air, / And the blue sky, and in the mind of man: / A motion and a spirit, that impels / All thinking things, all objects of all thought, / And rolls through all things."

2. Martha Heyneman. *The Breathing Cathedral: Feeling Our Way into a Living Cosmos* (San Francisco: Sierra Club Books, 1993).

3. As quoted in Martha Heyneman's *The Breathing Cathedral: Feeling Our Way into a Living Cosmos.*

4. Andre LaCocque. *The Trial of Innocence: Adam, Eve, and the Yahwist* (Eugene, OR: Wipf & Stock, 2006).

5. Paul Ricoeur and Andre LaCocque. *Thinking Biblically: Exegetical and Hermeneutical Studies* (Chicago, IL: University of Chicago Press. 1998). Quoted by Doug Thorpe in. *Wisdom Sings the World* (New York: Codhill, 2010).

6. In the Bible, the Hebrew word *shalom* refers to a state of wholeness, completion, and well-being, tranquility, prosperity, and security. It is a manifestation of Divine grace, of creation as it was meant to be.

7. Richard Wagner, in his essay "The Artwork of the Future," included in William Oliver Strunk's book *Source Readings in Music History*, vol.1 (New York: Norton, 1998), describes mu-

sic's "just measure" as "laws of harmonic succession, based on relationships." Aristotle applied the notion of a "just measure" to a far wider realm, saying that it exists for "the size of the city, as for everything else, animals, plants, organs." Barbara Cassin, in her book *Dictionary of Untranslatables: A Philosophical Lexicon* (Princeton, NJ: Princeton University Press, 2013), page 567, says the original Greek concept of a just measure was also linked to the idea of *kairos* as an opening in chronological time, through which order and action can emerge into the ordinary world of experience.

8. To read more about visionary teaching, see *Teaching with Vision: Culturally Responsive Teaching in Standards-Based Classrooms*, Christine E. Sleeter and Catherine Cornbleth, Catherine, eds. (New York: Teachers College Press, 2011).

9. Gary Snyder. *The Practice of the Wild* (New York: Farrar, Straus & Giroux, 1990).

10. Catherine Keller. *Face of the Deep: A Theology of Becoming* (London: Routledge, 2002).

11. James D. G. Dunn. *Jesus Remembered: Christianity in the Making* (Grand Rapids, MI: Eerdmans, 2003), page 225, quoting the works of C.F. Burney and Joachim Jeremias.

12. Madeleine L'Engle. *Walking on Water* (Wheaton, IL: H. Shaw, 1980), page 24.

When one reaches the highest degree of human maturity, one has only one question left: how can I be helpful?

-RONALD ROLHEISER
(ATTRIBUTED TO TERESA OF AVILA)

Into the Ordinary

Waypost 7

At the top of Mount Purgatory, Dante finds himself standing in front of a scorching wall of fire. He quivers with fear—but his path leads directly through the flames. There is no way around.

Virgil coaxes Dante forward by first entering the flames himself. Emboldened, Dante finally steps into the fire. The heat is so intense he wants to be drenched in molten glass just to cool off. In spite of the sensation of burning, however, he is physically unharmed. Not a single hair on his head is even singed.

When Dante emerges on the other side of the wall of fire, he's been cleansed, and the P's carved into his forehead at the beginning of the climb are all erased now. Virgil recognizes his apprentice's full spiritual maturity. Having learned to govern his appetites, and to direct his innate love toward the higher Good, Dante is now crowned and mitered, able to wisely govern both body and soul.

With full stature and agency, Dante leaves behind Virgil's intellectual reasoning as his guide. He is ready now to be initiated into the Divine community by the radiant Beatrice, symbol of sacred wisdom.

IMAGINE

As you continue on your journey, you take the path that emerges out of the forest into a clearing. Up ahead at the base of a mountain, a town's rooftops are alight in the full midday sun. Beyond the settlement are looming mountains.

Slowly, you make your way down the path toward the town. Ahead of you, distant figures approach along the snakelike trail, but for now, you are still alone. You hear the whisper of the breeze through the tall grass that lines your path. The sun is warm on your head.

As you come closer to the buildings ahead, you realize that the settlement is far larger than you first thought. Even from this distance, you can hear the din of voices and traffic, the interwoven sounds of many people going about their business. You cross a bridge over a small stream, enter by a gate in the wall, and find yourself in a city.

Shopkeepers haggle with patrons, tradespeople go about their work, farmers hand their produce from their carts. Somewhere, someone is chopping wood. Coins clink on the tables. Merchants scribble in ledger books. Chickens cluck and murmur, scratching in the dirt streets. A dog barks in the distance. Important-looking people hurry past. A monk loads his newly purchased goods onto a cart. Children laugh as they run to school. A beggar asks for alms. Wooden wheels creak over cobblestone, and horse hooves clop out a steady rhythm. Two merchants break into an argument.

You have entered a human space with its many systems of exchange, of law, of hierarchy, of money and power. Trying to take it all in, you are almost overwhelmed after the quiet of the abbey and the forest. This is a place of ambition, competition, and conflict—but also, you sense, of beauty, of community, of exchange and transformation.

Your gaze is drawn to a mountain just beyond the town, looming above the rooftops. On some inner level, you understand that this is your destination. Something there calls to you.

But first, here among the people of the city, you enjoy the energy of conversation, movement, exchange. A woman offers you an apple with a smile. You take it, find a place to sit on a bench at the edge of the town square, and eat.

So far on your journey home you have been engaged in a great deal of internal work. You've confronted the shadow, found rest, and reflected on what inspires you. But the inner journey also points us outward; it makes us more deeply aware of our interconnectedness with the world around us—the Earth, our community, our family.

Just as we both inhale and exhale, our very breath in dynamic relationship with our environment, so too our inner and outer work are linked together. On one side, we make space for play, for inspiration, for self-awareness. On the other side, we *act*, in tangible ways, contributing in some way to the external world. Our work is the contribution that connects us to the greater whole of which we are a part. In this chapter, we direct our attention outward.

For Dante, the ideal "kingdom"—what we might call "community"—protects us through the moral laws of love and grace. In a play on words, the Latin *Roma*, Dante's ideal community, is bound by love, which is *Roma* spelled in reverse: *Amor*. The healthy community is inextricably linked with the love that supports it.

Our task is to direct our love toward the greater good and in so doing, build community. We work toward greater healing and wholeness, not just for ourselves, but for all. Part of this shift in focus from self-centered, ego-driven pursuits to a life of genuine service for others involves dying to self. This takes deep self-recognition of who we are and who we are meant to be. It requires that we consent to being *ordinary*, recognizing our place, our part, within a greater order, rather than insisting on our prominence and importance.

My own experience in finding a sense of vocation moved along the path that Dante describes. Unlike most seminarians, I had attended seminary in hopes of becoming a writer rather than a clergyperson, because most writers I admired—Blake, Dostoevsky, Eliot—had a deeply theological imagination. My master's program focused on theology and the arts and was intended to inform my future work, which I believed would be poems, novels, screenplays.

There's something deeply satisfying in organizing ideas into a coherent form and finding language to articulate those ideas with specificity and precision. But in an unconscious state, the process can also contain a good deal of ego. If a metaphorical imagination is unique and rare in this day and age, I reasoned, what better way to distinguish myself than by going against the grain? I dreamed of getting recognition, even if only within a small circle. Writing seemed to me to be the introvert's means of fulfilling the need for approval and esteem, while still being socially isolated.

As I started to shape my ideas along these lines, however, trying my hand at novels and stories, I found the process slow and arduous. I was attempting social criticism with my writing, but the underlying energy came from a place of bitterness. As a result, my writing was not cultivating wholeness in the world.

I also realized I would need years of work before I could achieve any kind of quality and maturity in my writing. In the meantime, I would have to pay the bills. What I had thought would be my means to fulfillment had now become an obstacle.

Around the same time, I got married, in part to fulfill my need for companionship and affection. Instead, I started to feel trapped and alone, far from home, my wife working long and irregular hours as we struggled to get on the same page. Once again, what I had thought would be a route to fulfillment had become an obstacle.

Teaching, which can also be a means of looking for esteem and attention (after all, there's a captive audience), proved to be arduous and draining. Another obstacle to fulfillment. With a tight work schedule, even simple pleasures—like personal reading, travel, and time with close friends—were gone from my life. For the lover of pleasure having no access to pleasure can feel like a personal hell. I drank most nights and became irritable, angry, petulant, withdrawn. I felt my addictive behavior was justified by the demands of my life.

The myths touch on this pattern of becoming walled in by defensiveness. In one ancient tale, for instance, King Minos of Crete receives a gift from the god Poseidon, a magnificent white bull, intended as a sacrifice to honor the god. Instead of sacrificing the bull, however, Minos keeps it. As punishment, Poseidon causes Minos's wife Pasiphae to fall madly in love with the bull. She mates with it, and the result is the monstrous Minotaur. The craftsman Daedalus creates a labyrinth precisely as a means of hiding the monstrosity, the consequence of distorted desire. In the classical version of the story, Theseus is the hero who enters the labyrinth and kills the Minotaur; when the labyrinth was adopted by medieval Christians as a symbol of the journey of faith and Divine transformation, Christ became the hero. In this version of the story, our own defensiveness and resistance is the "labyrinth" that hides the monstrosity within, and through Christ—through surrender, sacrifice, and the death of the self—we become transformed. The hinge of this transformation, the inflection point, is self-recognition. We must see *who we truly are*.[1]

The spiritual journey is not a surrogate route to fulfilling our desires with Divine help. Instead, it's a dislocation of the ego that would otherwise keep us from seeing the truth of things. It's a change in how we perceive. From this new perspective, we see a greater pattern and order, of which we are a part. We are ordinary.

Ordinary shares its root—the Latin *ordo*—with the word *order*. To be ordinary is simply to recognize one's place as a part of that greater pattern. This is already the case, whether we dwell in that awareness of not, but the ego bucks against this reality. It wants differentiation, significance through distinction; it longs to feel superior in some way. Only as we let go of that craving can we come back to ourselves, in relationship to others and in relationship to the greater whole. This recognition subverts the normal concepts, categories, and labels we use to navigate the world. It becomes a channel for love. But first, like Dante penetrating the wall of fire, we have to overcome the obstacles the ego has built up, its attachments and desires.

The most basic kind of love Dante refers to early in his story is the love of pleasure. This low-level love can lead to vice. Through the refining process along the path of Mount Purgatory, he learns the discipline and will required to move from vice to virtue, from indulgence to surrender.

That progression corresponds to my own experience in teaching, in marriage, in parenthood, and in my own addictions. These experiences became my teachers, my guides. Instead of pushing back against these experiences when they failed to be fulfilling or give pleasure, I learned to direct my attention toward them. The question became, "How can I be of service in this situation, *through* this situation? How can I manifest love-in-action here and now?" And when unconsciousness, ego, anger, resentment, and self-centeredness crept back in, as they always do, I learned to watch that, observe it, understand where it comes from, and extend grace to myself as someone who is still on the path. This turning from ego to love redeems the entire journey, the building of obstacles, even addiction itself. On Dante's road, even the path through Hell is part of the journey of transformation, just as Dante climbed down on the scales of Satan himself as part of his precise path toward wisdom.

But now, in Dante's Purgatory, suffering is collective rather than isolated. Unlike Hell, here the sinners suffer together. There's a sense of community. The threads of union, of community and connection, weave through these cantos of the poem as both friends and enemies are reunited in Purgatory.

And when Dante passes through the final wall of flame that purifies the soul, he is reunited with

Beatrice, the woman who has long been the object of his desire. Here, though, his desire is transfigured. This particular woman, the human woman Dante has loved and yearned for throughout his life, is the vehicle through which Dante comes into a greater understanding of the Divine, an experiential grasp of Divine love far deeper than Virgil's intellectual reason could ever impart. Through Beatrice, Dante understands that his selfish desire for a specific beloved must die in order for it to blossom into a selfless desire for the Divine. His desire for Beatrice is no longer directed toward either the fulfillment of individual longing or earthly lust, but has become a lesson in the true object of *all* desire—Divine union. Dante's encounter with Beatrice is a picture of desire redeemed; desire recognizes its true object, which is in fact no object at all, but self-transcendence.

That's what the labyrinth is all about as well, and that's what pilgrimage is about: realigning our desire, redirecting it from the temporal to the transcendent. Instead of having the limited appetites of the False Self fulfilled, our eyes are opened in recognition. We recognize ourselves, we see the games we habitually play, and we surrender to a process of transformation. We are known, given purpose, and find transformation in community. There's a sense of *homecoming*.

In the earthly Paradise at the top of Mount Purgatory, Beatrice speaks of the community that awaits Dante at the end of the Paradiso. Her goal is to prepare him for that community. The work she gives him as a poet is to tell difficult truths, to communicate for the edification of others through his poem. He then has a symbolic vision of the tribulation of the Church throughout history.[2] Dante's role in bringing healing to the greater body is to represent these truths accurately back to the reader. In writing the poem itself, he's living out his vocation. He's both communicating and living truth.

The mythical journey is about learning from trials, experiencing transformation, then bringing this newfound insight and wisdom *back to the community* to bring about restoration there. We've learned that there is no rebirth without death, but this transformation is not ours alone. We exist in community.

The traditional metaphor for the interdependent community is the body. In his *Republic*, Plato speaks of "the body politic" to describe society as a political unity, while in the New Testament, Paul writes of the spiritual community as "the body of Christ." As pilgrims following Dante's road, we too are called to bring healing in whatever way we can to the body of which we are a part. The journey home asks that we see beyond our limited selves, and even beyond our immediate tribes, to the healing of the greater community.

The great stories touch on this truth in their own ways. In dealing with the suitors who have plagued his home for years, Homer's Odysseus, for example, restores order to his both his home *and* his entire kingdom on the island of Ithaca. The common plot device of ending a story in a marriage or with the birth of a child represents new life and hope for the future of the entire community. The mythical journey is not about individual healing alone, but about the process of transforming society, transforming the world, into wholeness, into *shalom*.

In our time, this interconnectedness is inescapable. The world economy is intertwined as never before. Problems in one market affect the rest of the world. Global climate change is a constant reminder that our consumption patterns and daily practices have disastrous effects on others. This broader awareness of the consequences of our own actions on others and the discipline to bring about change is one characteristic of the spiritual maturity we're seeking. Given these realities, a question with which we are faced as we continue on our journey is that of *vocation*.

IMAGINE

As you sit at the edge of the town square, consider the hands that designed and built the houses and towers around you. As you remember the abbey and the farms you passed, bring to your consciousness the work of the monks and the farmers in the fields. Recall the work of the ants in the forest—and now look around you at the work of the merchants, the craftspeople, the officials, each a part of a greater whole.

Pause for a moment and take some time to reflect: what is your work in the world?

One way to analyze this question is to define the word itself: *work* is action that influences the world around us. The question becomes, then: in what way do *you* influence the world? In what way do you *want* to?

Any specific and concrete answer to this question is inherently limited. Whether we want to build boats or buildings or businesses, all these things will fade in time. Like all forms, given a long enough timeline, both our physical bodies and the physical fruits of our labor will fade away. What remains is the energy we put into the world, the dynamics we set into motion, through our interaction with others and with the land. When we are gone, what quality of energy will have increased in the world? Answering this question helps orient us on our path. It points us in the direction we need to go.

Another way to ask this question is: how will you help move the community toward greater wholeness? In the previous chapter, we took an oblique approach to this question, speaking of creativity and play, which is how we stay in touch with the generative source, how we stay inspired. What are the experiences in which we are able to lose ourselves, during which we have the greatest sense of attunement with the world around us? The purpose of these experiences is not merely our own pleasure, for we are also called to give back, to participate in the ongoing process of a wider transformation.

Look back at what you learned about yourself in the cave; there is likely some connection between the core need you identified and the work to which you are called. This work may be your daily job, the way in which you make a living—or it may not.

On the one hand, if we have learned our lesson on the mythical path, we experience a deep sense of orientation, a state of being in the world that we bring to whatever daily tasks in which we engage, giving meaning to the most ordinary of tasks. At the same time, we also want our daily work to align more directly with our sense of values, drive, and purpose. We want a sense of vitality, which is an outcome of dynamic participation.

We may not feel that at this moment our job and our vocation are well matched, but if we develop what psychologist Carol Dweck calls a "growth mindset,"[3] we will understand that none of us are in a fixed state but are always developing. This allows us to be patient with the reality of our life, while at the same time we accept new challenges, even if we don't feel prepared for them. We become open to process and figuring out solutions as we go along.

The same mindset also allows us grace and patience with others, as we are able to see each partner, colleague, friend, and family member as works-in-progress. Where the people in our lives fall short, we may even become agents of change in their lives, inasmuch as we see through their behaviors to the underlying causes. We see their pain, their fear, and their misunderstanding; and where appropriate, we can speak and act compassionately in their lives, seeing potential where others don't.

As we make this shift from ego mechanisms rooted in our core wounds to a sense of agency and inner purpose, our core needs will also be transformed. If the core need of our False Self is *stability and security*, then becoming more and more aware of our own thoughts, emotions, and behavior patterns can lead to a core strength of *stewardship*. We go from looking for protection to finding ways to genuinely protect and preserve. We shift from trying to fulfill a core need to a desire for outward service. We move from self-centered to other-centered lives. If our core need has been *affection and esteem*, our inner work may lead us to develop a core strength of *healing and care*. Rather than looking to fulfill our own deep emotional needs, we help others heal emotionally. And finally, if our core need has been *power and control*, once we begin to process and grow toward maturity, we will likely develop a core strength of *empowerment*, speaking encouragement and inspiration into the lives of others, helping to motivate and elevate them to become the fullest expression of their True Self. Undertaking the mental exercise of identifying our core strength and core purpose not only roots us more firmly in our true identities; it also helps us make decisions and act in ways that are more in line with our values.

In this conscious state, we are open to what is. Infused with spirit, we are free to pursue our sense of external purpose without the need for personal gain or ego fulfillment. Of course, the desires for status, affection, and stability don't disappear, but once we're aware of them, we don't have to *identify* with them. We let them come and go. We identify with the much deeper dimension of spirit, like a tree rooted in firm soil, or as Jesus says, "like a house built upon the rock."[4] First, though, to establish this firm foundation, we have to dig down and find the bedrock deep beneath the soil.

Pursuing conscious vocation means we understand any obstacles we encounter are transient. When we stop acting out of unconsciousness, life begins to mysteriously unfold for us. We ride it like a wave rather than standing still and being battered by the waves.

In my own life, I lived for years in a state of inner resistance to my surroundings that sapped much of my energy and vitality. I held a ravenous unconscious need for affection and esteem that could not possibly be addressed in my profession or in my marriage, or not nearly to the degree I felt I needed. Every day felt like a new accumulation of insufficiencies and resentments. I *resented* that I didn't have time to immerse myself in literature and poetry, much less be creative, even though that was simply the consequence of having a full-time job. I *resented* that I didn't have time or energy (let alone talent) to write and record music, again a luxury few working adults have. My emotional well-being felt as though it were nowhere near as important to my wife as I thought it should be, and she became the most available target onto which to project my issues. After years of trying, we couldn't get pregnant, and it seemed like even God had no interest in keeping me happy—and so I *resented* being denied a family. My needy ego was being whittled away, and the enormous amount of daily inner resistance to the reality around me only made things that much more painful.

I felt impotent on almost every level: unable to live out calling, unable to be effective, unable to have a family, and most important from the ego's perspective, unable to receive the kind of affection and esteem I needed to feel alive at all. I felt trapped. I lay awake at night and tried to understand how I'd gotten into this cycle of negativity, despite the best of intentions. All too often, however, I focused on the past, rather than identifying what inner changes might need to happen *now* for new growth. I romanticized past life situations as far more fulfilling.

Anger and rigidity set in. With no apparent way out of the layers of entrapment, I had regular thoughts of escape, of finding affection in other ways, of divorce, sometimes even of suicide. (After all, I reasoned, how likely was any other situation to be truly fulfilling?) Then I'd feel guilty about these thought patterns, adding to the inner weight on my spirit. Christ's invitation of a light yoke, of life abundant,[5] felt like an elaborate practical joke when I considered my life: the emptiness of my diligence, my Christian education, my graduate degree, my job, and my marriage. The message of my entire life seemed to be this: *you're a complete failure.*

When I committed to a daily contemplative practice, these ego structures began to crack. The changes were small and gradual at first, but slowly, I came to recognize that my own inner resistance to the world was partly what made it such a hostile place. I began to have enough perspective to *see* the dynamics in play: stress and resentment, insecurity and addiction. With ongoing contemplative practice, the walls within me began to fall, one by one. There was room now for grace to enter the picture. I registered where my daily frustrations came from, what I was responding to with negativity and anger, what made me long for a different kind of life, what made me react with pettiness. With this awareness came an opening for right action. As the monstrous ego began to shrink, I had more room in my perception for others, for their needs and for ways I might contribute to their growth. Now, my work came out of a different place.

I spent a year and a half integrating this newfound awareness into daily life. I observed my physical and emotional responses to stressors and simply watched. I asked where the reactions came from. Instead of ending each week with an accumulation of stress, resentment, frustration, and anger, I could watch it, feel it, and let it go. The next step was to observe my mental dialogue in response to frustrating situations or a harsh word. I became aware of this mental process, felt it, and also let it go. With no need to fight back, get even, or make sure at least someone else felt the pain I was feeling, I experienced an unburdening.

Taking this radical responsibility for my inner state eventually led to changes in my external life as well. I was asked to become a department chair at work. Soon after that, I was invited to take an out-of-class coordinatorship and consider a career in administration. Then my wife was offered a position in a different city that had a much more tight-knit community and slower pace of life. I traveled four hours back and forth on the weekends, and she traveled up to see me on her days off. Shortly after that, she found out she was pregnant. I found a position in the same city where she was working, and I was present for the birth of my son. Next, I got an at-home work position, allowing me to spend mornings with my family. In a short amount of time, my world had changed drastically.

Of course this shift wasn't instantaneous. The lives we lead out of ego have a certain momentum that can't be turned around immediately—but the inner journey makes room for positive change to occur. The light yoke and the abundant life occur when we've let go of the ego projects, illusions, and attachments that underpin our striving. This is why Jesus says it is easier for a camel to pass through the eye of a needle than for the rich man to enter the Kingdom[6]—because the rich man is unwilling to let go of his attachments, of his misguided program for happiness. But bringing our unconscious processes to light allows us to let them go.

For many of us, this only occurs after we've suffered enough from our ego pursuits that we're sick and tired of being sick and tired. Only then are we finally ready to let go. This creates an opening where our internal purpose can emerge into our external lives, as we move from ego-driven projects to genuine *other-centered lives.*

Dante learns something of this process on his climb up the mountain. An inversion of Hell, the levels of Purgatory are organized by varying degrees of perverted, deficient, or misdirected love. Virgil had explained to him that on this mountain the process of purgation makes the climb less difficult as it goes on, even as the path becomes steeper. The change is within the climber. As the understanding of the transformative purpose of suffering becomes clearer, the pilgrim is more willing to endure the difficulties of the upward climb. The importance of this image for our sense of vocation is clear: if we establish a sense of clear direction and purpose, the difficulties no longer keep us bogged down or hinder us from making progress. When we know precisely where we're headed and why, all obstacles are temporary.

IMAGINE

The midday sun is high overhead. You drink from a fountain and refill your water skin. You give a coin to a beggar. You speak to a merchant whose cart is stuck on the roadside, and then you find the wheelwright who follows you back to the merchant's cart to repair the broken wheel.

You notice that the noise of the day's business has died down. As you gaze up at the mountain, you feel its call, and you turn toward the road that leads out of the city. You are ready now to resume your journey.

As you make your way to the path that curls up the mountain, the slope grows steeper. At first, you climb easily, the sun pleasantly warm on your head and shoulders. For a moment, you pause to look back at the town where it lies below in the afternoon quiet. Then you walk on.

After a time, you pass a broad ledge just to the left of the path. A man stands there, teaching several people who are sitting around him. You notice, but you do not stop.

Farther up the mountainside, the climb becomes steeper and narrower, and now your legs are beginning to tire and sweat drips down your face. When you turn around and pause for a few breaths, the city is far, far below, so distant that the buildings look like a child's toys. You realize that as you pursue an internal call, you've left behind the comforts of civilization, its rhythms and order.

As you resume the climb, your path leads you over ledges and around sharp curves, and you breathe heavily, your muscles straining. At the same time, though, you feel a growing sense of exhilaration, and your feet move faster. Finally, you reach the mountaintop and pause there, taking in deep breaths of the clear air.

The sun has sunk lower in the sky, and the first shadows of late afternoon stretch across the mountainside, while the day's heat surrenders to a cooler breeze. As you look out over the valley below, the light fades into orange, with touches of violet, crimson, and gold on the clouds. From your lofty vantage point, you see the village at the mountain's base, the fields, the abbey, and the forest beyond. Far in the distance, you can even make out the jagged rocks around the mouth of the cave you left behind.

You consider the work you have observed throughout the day—the monks, the ant and earthworm, the farmer, the tradespeople, the shopkeepers—each part of a larger system, and these systems in turn part of still larger systems. Your muscles pleasantly tired, you acknowledge your own hard work as you have journeyed. As you watch, the sun sets on this single day's work.

Have you ever had the experience of standing outside the world's workings and seeing its interconnectedness? There is elegance in the interlocking parts making up the whole, even while there's a simultaneous destructive energy of injustice, exploitation, domination, inequality, greed, and selfishness. In a mature spiritual state, we can begin to realize the links between the world within and the world without. Our ability to help move society toward wholeness is in direct relationship to our awareness of our own wounds and selfish patterns, as well as our ability to allow ourselves the grace for change.

As we follow our own calling, our service in the world, however, we can do as much harm as good if we remain unconscious of our ego. One way to avoid this is to pay attention to the work we are doing, to notice our relationship to the work itself. As we do, we will become more and more aware that as we go further on our inner journey, we learn to *serve* the work.

Some of the most accomplished workers in their respective fields, whether music, medicine, research, or athletics, identify a point of selflessness, of flow. In the

Eastern tradition this is called *wu wei*, or "no mind"—being completely focused and attentive to the requirements of the moment. This is complete immersion in something larger than ourselves, and it is here that we often have a foretaste of what the contemplatives call egolessness.

Without practicing awareness, however, we will return to ego mind when we move on to other tasks, other business. Even now on our journey, after we have come so far—done the difficult work of the downward climb, uncovered our core need—we realize the inner work is not finished. We are ascending now, though, rather than descending.

Here, as we approach the mountaintop of our spirit, we find an exhilaratingly expansive vision. The obstacles to our vision are removed, and we can see in every direction. No wonder that mountain imagery is so prevalent in spiritual language!

IMAGINE

You stand for a few moments on the mountaintop, your spirit soaring with exhilaration. But soon, you notice a new mystery.

A short distance away, three hooded figures sit in silence around a fire. As you watch, they look up and notice you—and then they stand up and walk toward you. . . .

WAYPOST 7 EXERCISES

Select **at least two** exercises:

1. **Vocation:** What would you be if money, education, and time were no object? Acrobat? News anchor? Astronaut? List five careers. What is it about these jobs that seems fulfilling to you? Write down what they have in common. Now compare these roles to what you're already doing. Are there any changes to be made? Small ones? Big ones?

2. **Observing:** Go to a public square, visit your downtown, or take a ride on public transportation in your city—and simply observe. If you live in a more rural area, go to some function where people are congregated. As you watch people, do you notice a clear need or desire in them? Write a journal entry describing the experience.

3. **Work Preference Reflection:** On a sheet of paper, reflect on three jobs, positions, or activities in which you've been formally involved. For each position, write down what it was, when you performed it, three aspects of it you enjoyed, your favorite memory from this time, and three aspects of it you didn't

enjoy; then give the overall experience a grade. Look for patterns in your likes and dislikes of the work. What type of work are you drawn toward? What are you repelled by? You may find surprising answers.

4. **The Letter:** Write a letter to yourself at the age of ten about that child's dreams for the future. If they've changed drastically, how so? Why did they change?

5. **Visio Divina:** Take a close look at the paintings *Politics, Law, and Farming in Missouri* by Thomas Hart Benton, *The Milkmaid* by Johannes Vermeer, and *Haystacks* by Claude Monet. Research the background of these paintings. Consider the labor depicted or implied and the various kinds of transformation at work. Write a reflection on the painting that speaks to you most.

6. **Poetica Divina:** Read the poems "Digging" by Seamus Heaney, "Musée Des Beaux Arts" by W.H. Auden, and "Simone Weil: The Year of Factory Work (1934–1935)" by Edward Hirsch.

7. **Audio Divina:** Listen to a song that invokes a sense of sacred or redeemed work for you. (My selections: "Work the Black Seam" by Sting, "My Hometown"

by Bruce Springsteen, or "Making Pies" by Patty Griffin.)

8. **Family Work:** Consider the work of your family members, your grandparents, your parents, your siblings. Describe the work they did or do now. What qualities did they or do they now bring into the world through their work? Consider both the positive and negative elements. Which of these qualities would you like to bring into the world? How?

9. **Lectio Divina:** Ecclesiastes 3:18–22 (Read, Reflect, Respond, *Rest*).

NOTES

1. Thorpe, Doug. *Wisdom Sings the World: Poetry, Creation, and the Way of Dwelling* (New York: Codhill Press, 2010), pages 138–147.

2. An eagle attacks the chariot that carries Beatrice, a fox enters it and gnaws at it from within—and then comes the eagle again, leaving some feathers behind. Finally, a dragon emerges from the ground, tears away a piece of the chariot, and makes off with it. The eagle feathers left behind begin to fester, and the chariot transforms into a monster that is dragged into the forest by a giant. Commentaries on *The Divine Comedy* suggest that this is an elaborate allegory of attacks on the Church both from without and within throughout history. These images are thought to represent

the persecution of the Church by the Roman Empire, then the division caused by heresy, then a second attack on the Church, this time from within after the dispensation under Constantine that caused corruption within the Church, here figured as a kind of schism. The defiled Church devolves into a monstrosity.

3. Carol S. Dweck. *Mindset: The New Psychology of Success* (New York: Random House, 2006).

4 Luke 6:46–48.

5. "My yoke is easy, and my burden is light" (Matthew 11:30) and "I am come that they might have life, and that they might have *it* more abundantly" (John 10:10).

6. Matthew 19:24.

The love of Christ is a force for transformation, an agent of transfomation, and a challenge to metanoia—a word often anemically translated as repentance or conversion, but which in the original Greek has a much richer meaning of "changing your mind" or perhaps more accurately "adopting a new consciousness."

–CARL McCOLMAN

The victory of God means the defeat of the ego. The defeat of all egocentric narratives. God does not become victorious through some effort. God is always already victorious. But that victory is only recognized when the ego's helplessness and the futility of establishing the reality of any ego is recognized.

–SHUNYAMURTI

PART THREE

THE UPWARD GAZE

Only after we have let go of ourselves will we be able, in a state of inner detachment, to gain peace and the "fullness of divine being." Only then will we attain a detachment that is much more than just an outward gesture of release, since it effects an inner transformation and "purity of heart," for "blessed are the pure in heart, for they shall see God."

–WOLFGANG KOPP

We walk the labyrinth or go on pilgrimage, and that walking takes us to a literal end or center. But the center of the labyrinth is not only a literal place into which we walk by our own volition; it's also a metaphorical place that we enter mysteriously by grace, through surrender. It does not come unless we give ourselves to it. We do not create this place; we do not control it. It comes to us like love.

–DOUG THORPE

Into Emptiness

Waypost 8

At the top of Mount Purgatory, Dante is confronted with creation's highest beauty, surpassed only by the beauty of his childhood love, Beatrice, who is radiant in her Divine splendor. As Dante stands before her now, his eyes are downcast in shame. His gaze darts about, and tears begin to fall. When he catches a glimpse of his reflection in the river, he feels even worse and turns away from his own image. Beatrice scolds him in order to reorient him.

He realizes that in his youth, when he first encountered Beatrice's gentle beauty, his love for her was a guiding light, a moral compass that shaped and cultivated the quality of virtue in his poetic talent. But after she died, he became disoriented. He started misusing his talents—to become famous, to pursue counterfeit beauty, to celebrate earthly lust and misguided desire. She then came to him in dreams to steer him back to his true course, but her advice went unheeded, and he continued in his error and aimlessness. He wandered so far off track that she had to send a guide—Virgil—to walk with Dante through the fires of Hell so that he could find his way again.

Moved by her words, Dante confesses through his tears that he had indeed been lured by false beauty, by fame, by pride, and by lust. Beatrice commands Dante to look straight at her, to hold her in his gaze, to amplify his sense of burning shame—what today we might call a sense of cognitive dissonance between our ideals and our reality—by looking at true beauty.

Beatrice then turns to the Griffin, a mythical creature of two natures—human and Divine—and as she looks at him, her beauty grows more astounding in Dante's eyes until, feverish and overwhelmed, he collapses in a faint. When he wakes up, Beatrice tell him to immerse himself in the river Lethe, the river of forgetting. Because of his self-honesty, his transgressions are washed away in the water: he will forget what he has done and the shame it has caused him.

Submerged in the water, he hears the words of the Latin antiphon *"Asperges Me"*—cleanse me—being sung from the shore.[1] Still floating deep in the river, Dante is invited into the dance of four nymphs in a Divine procession. Now, he finds he is able to turn his gaze to Beatrice and her radiant beauty without shame. To empower him even more, Beatrice commands him to be dipped into the river Eunoe, the river of memory, and now his own acts of virtue come flooding back to him. He's restored to his true self, fully purged, fully cleansed of broken memories, fully empowered by virtuous awareness, and is now ready for his journey into the celestial Paradise.

In the last two chapters, we took a look at different ways in which we can contribute to the world around us through creativity and meaningful work in the world. We want to move the world toward wholeness. But now we come to a limitation—*our very own selves*. Like Dante, when we are finally forced to face our own image, we realize the distance between our ideals and our reality.

And yet we have already traveled so far on Dante's road. We have confronted our inner ego desires, articulated our inner purpose, and set out with zeal and fervor . . . only to find after a time of contribution and community that new wounds are inflicted, both by us and upon us. Our ego patterns, insecurities, and unconscious anxieties rear their old familiar heads, limiting our effectiveness, constraining our lives. They can also become triggers for those around us, whose own ego-energy responds negatively to ours. We find ourselves with what we feel is unnecessary resistance, competition, and hostility, usually from *within* our own community, workplace, or tribe.

As a result, we may go through periods of ineffectiveness and a sense of distance in our relationships, with our true effectiveness sliding into languor on the one side or overzealous ambition on the other. At the same time that we register successes, we may also experience broken relationships and burnt bridges. We might find ourselves using people unconsciously to achieve our ends or demonizing those we perceive as working against our stated inner purpose. As we fall into projection, anger, attack, and distorted vision—often with external support from our chosen community—we once more exist in a state of unconsciousness or spiritual adolescence. Despite all our spiritual growth, we have slammed once more against the limitations of our ways of knowing. We have run full tilt into the obstacles of the ego, which is so persistent.

At this level, what we struggle against is a confused or distorted set of priorities. Throughout our entire lives the outer or external reality that exists in our mental perceptions has been given exaggerated primary importance. As a result, we may follow spiritual tenets, enjoy a community of faith of whatever stripe, develop deep compassion for others, and engage in impactful work, and still find ourselves struggling with our ego patterns. This can be difficult to realize once we have made what we feel are life-altering decisions for growth, especially if we adopted an expression of faith. We may have a new language, new practices, a new community, and in many ways a new life—but soon, conflicts arise even here.

A Divine longing calls us to become more than this limited self with its ongoing dramas. Overcoming this limitation, however, requires continued effort as we undertake the mythical journey. Dante's road is a mystical path that transcends the rational and moves us into the dark heart of love. It asks that we make the ascent toward what the mystics call *theosis*, or *Divine union*. This is the third stage of the spiritual journey.

The fourth-century Church father Athanasius said, "God became human so that human could become God." The literal mind registers this statement only as a kind of overreach, a hyperbole, but a deeper process is at work beneath the surface bombast of the statement. The obstacle separating our humanity and our Divinity is what is described in mythical terms as our fallen nature, the flesh, or our limited egoic consciousness, the False Self. The mystics and contemplatives from ancient to modern times indicate that continually and intentionally releasing this aspect of ourselves opens us to the inflow of the Divine. It makes Divine union possible.

This process of refinement and transformation does not mean we become God in an absolute sense. Instead, we become increasingly stripped of the ego and so gradually ever more open to and aligned with the transcendent Divine reality which is everywhere present. This requires an intentionality, a consent to the Divine presence, a receptivity, a humility. It often comes after great loss opens up a space within us. Often our central struggle will come into sharp focus as we learn to let go even more completely than ever before, to the point of self-dissolution. It also usually requires some kind of ongoing, disciplined practice to maintain and expand this inner space of receptivity, of growing awareness.

In this space, we recognize we are partakers in the Divine nature in the deepest part of our being, our inmost self. As our awareness of this reality grows, we become more and more identified with this transcendent truth-in-process, and less identified with our small, egoic False Self and its programs for happiness.

This is the focus of the final part of our journey. It requires a sense of orientation, an attentiveness to our inner state and to external reality. It demands awareness and acceptance. It asks for letting go and receptivity.

It requires an upward gaze.

IMAGINE

On your own journey, you stand here at the top of the mountain as the day turns into evening and the first stars emerge overhead. The three men in robes and cowls come closer. Their gait is slow, their steps measured. Long shadows extend behind them, staining grass and rock and thistle with darkness.

Your eyes are drawn to the first man, who leads this small procession. He removes his cowl and smiles at you, and you see that his head is bald and his face lined. Despite his worn and craggy features, his gaze holds a soft openness, as if in recognition, as if he'd been waiting—not for just anyone but for you in particular. He doesn't speak but after a quiet moment, he extends his arm, placing into your hands a leather-bound book. He still says nothing. Then he and the other men each nod at you, as though in farewell, and begin to make their way back down the mountain path.

You walk over to the fire where the men were sitting and turn the book over in your hands, running your fingers across its leather surface. It has a golden clasp, which is locked. You cannot open the book to see what wisdom it may hold.

As the twilight deepens into night, the air grows cooler. You move closer to the fire and hug your clothing tight around you. After a moment, you accept that for now you cannot open this book, though you sense that it must be important to your journey. You place the book down on the ground beside you, take a deep breath, and relax as you watch the dancing flames. The fire's warmth creeps over you.

When the fire begins to die, you notice that the previous travelers left some wood behind. You put on another log and feel the warmth on your face as the flames lick the wood. A few sparks sputter up into the night air. In the distance, crickets begin their shrill chatter. More stars appear on the horizon.

The air is colder now, but the fire keeps you warm. As you listen to the quiet sounds and watch the ever-changing pattern of flame and spark, your mind wanders. You find yourself smiling as you recall the warm, familiar presence of the strangers as they handed you the book.

Suddenly, unexpectedly, a long shiver runs down your spine. The warmth and familiarity give way to scenes of dread from the past, memories that fill you with guilt, embarrassment, a sense of impotence, shame. The emotional response varies in degree, but at its core it is the same: there are still parts of you that you don't want to have exposed, to be seen. These are the times you failed or were beaten or shamed; when you continued to act out your old addictions, when you were caught or belittled, rejected, or abandoned. Even though you have grown in your awareness of your ego mechanisms, these pictures and feelings still exert power over you. The pattern of thinking of which they are a part is still seductive, and you are tempted to identify with these emotions, to see yourself as a victim.

This is an old familiar burden, but now, after you have come so far, its weight seems even greater. You did the difficult work of confronting your False Self back in the cave, and yet you find that this old negative energy is not gone completely. Your mind seems to spin out of control as you're pulled this way and that, bombarded by the images of fear, and by the desire to escape or to get revenge.

You see the people you've hurt. Those who have hurt you. A parent rages. Someone you love is crying. An enemy is gloating. The face of someone you betrayed hardens into disgust. The pornography is found on the computer. The emails from a lover are discovered. The bottles in the trash can are uncovered. The drugs are found in the underwear drawer. The car crash plays back through your mind. You relive the arrest. The memories swirl with a feverish intensity. A rejection in childhood. A lover's final letter.

The fire that just moments ago was a comforting warmth now seems to grow and wrap you in its raging flames. The voices from the past mingle with the crackle of the fire, growing in volume until they become a deafening roar. *You are worthless. You are nothing. All your efforts are in vain. They never loved you. You will never amount to anything. Everything you do is tainted by your guilt, your sin, your shame.*

Then precisely here, in this moment, in this place where you are enveloped by fire, a tiny space opens up within your mind. You hear a small voice beneath the din, a gentle voice that does not condemn you. You remember that this happened before, in the cave, and so now, here on the mountaintop, you hear the voice more readily than you did before. It brings you a sliver of awareness. *This isn't you*, it tells you softly. *Don't fight. Don't run. Simply bear witness.*

Ever so gently, you begin to slip into another level of awareness, guided by the quiet voice. As if from the outside, you watch the images, the faults, the fear, the shame; you see them now as if they're happening to someone else. You feel compassion for this person's suffering, the strictures and mental chains, even though they're yours.

All the things you've done. All the things done to you. You hold them both as if in the palm of your hand, but you no longer identify with them. Instead, you clearly see how your False Self is generated by your original wound, and by the accumulated thoughts and responses, the patterns and choices and friendships and group identities and conditioning and addictions and justifications that layer over top that wound. You have gone this way before, back in the cave, and so the struggle to do so is less this time. You already know the way to go.

Now, you are moved to compassion even for those who hurt you in their own ignorance and unconsciousness. You call to mind the most painful of these relationships. Those who have hurt you the most. You look into their faces and allow yourself to see, even feel, the pain and shame from these past experiences. Then you speak words of forgiveness to them, one by one. Next, you remember the faces of those you have hurt. You ask them forgiveness, each in turn.

Gradually, the images dissolve. Their voices fade into silence. The roaring flame that threatened to consume you shrinks back into the flickering campfire. You realize that what seemed to have been a terrifying inferno was actually a sacred flame. It was not threatening to consume you but rather it was burning away all that was false.

This is revelation. This is awareness. This identity you've fashioned—this social self with a face and a name and a nationality and a reputation—is not who you ultimately are. You have a deeper, inner self, connected to Divinity. This is the immortal diamond.

As you let fall the attachments that keep you bound, you allow the False Self to dissolve more and more. This is a process that may take a lifetime, but you know now what you have to do to. You shift your awareness from the small everyday self with its wants, needs, and regrets to this transcendent, timeless, inner self. You see through the eyes of its pure grace.

Here at this milestone on Dante's road, we begin to see we are engaged in an ongoing process of transformation and refinement, of disidentification with the small self, of letting go, of *dying* to selfishness. This is our task in this chapter: to recognize the ongoing need to pay attention to the ego at work, the need to continually and intentionally let our ego die in order to move from False Self to True Self.

We have come to understand the ego processes at work in us and in the world, but the ongoing work of *paying attention* and *letting go* remain. This is the daily work. In Christian terminology, this is what it means to follow Jesus, to pick up our cross and walk. If we don't engage in this ever-evolving work of paying attention and tilling our internal soil, of conscious surrender, the relentless ego mechanisms will take over once more. We will once again be bogged down in the same patterns of self-doubt and fear, or we'll fall victim to old patterns of addiction and apathy. Whatever progress we've made on the spiritual journey can come to feel like a distant dream or a failure after all, another empty pursuit, rather than lasting transformation. But this is the spiritual work. It is a normal process, and it does not mean we have failed, or that our earlier experiences of inner awareness were false. At this waypost we attend to those inner dynamics on the ground level. We examine how these processes manifest in our day-to-day lives.

Within the Christian tradition, the theological term for this process is *kenosis*, or self-emptying. When speaking of the same concept, a Buddhist might refer to *shunyata*.[2] St. Paul's words in Philippians invites us to "let this mind be in you which was also in Christ Jesus: Who, existing in the form of God, did not consider equality with God something to be grasped, but emptied Himself."[3] The words *emptied himself* here in the original Greek derive from the term *kenosis*. In this simple but profound act of first noticing and then releasing our moment-to-moment ego processes, we make room for Divine transformation.

After several years of a daily contemplative practice—of sitting in attentive silence, letting thoughts go and consenting to the Divine presence and action within—I became more attuned to daily stressors and my responses to them. The discipline asked that I simply notice what was happening as it happened, without judging it or adding another layer of commentary and resistance.

Teaching, for example, is inherently stressful. There is always too much to accomplish in too short a time, and corralling students and their attention spans was an art in itself. Many times during the school day, I'd find myself responding in anger to interruptions in the lessons I had so carefully planned. Announcements over the intercom, students late to class, counselors pulling students out, TAs from the administrative office bringing notifications and summonses several times a period, students' phones going off, students' complaining, all threatened on a regular basis the delicate flow of my teaching. This meant I was agitated and irritable nearly constantly.

My natural bent is toward ideas, emotions, memories, imagination. To stay focused on practical goals in the immediate environment takes a high degree of discipline and attention—so when I engaged in careful planning toward a practical goal and then experienced an onslaught of obstacles to realistically achieving it, I was inevitably frustrated. And yet, after engaging so long in my contemplative practice, I understood that my irritation, my anger, and my unskillful responses were my own responsibility. I could no longer blame others for my frustration; it was up to me alone to inspect the source of the anger and then deal with it. This was not easy, since my reactions had many layers, many threads, which were difficult to track. In the moment, an inciting incident might register simply as a straw that broke the camel's back. A daily contemplative practice, however, helped me be more vigilant, noticing the small stressors throughout the day as they built up, rather than being taken by surprise by the final frustration that tipped me over the edge.

Contemplative practice is just that—*practice*. As we set aside daily time to practice noticing our thoughts, memories, and emotions as they arise, this soon bleeds over into everyday life, where we would otherwise take our emotional responses to be inevitable. In my case, my regular ongoing daily practice allowed me to eventually see the processes at work as *they were happening*.

That didn't happen immediately, though. At first, after some practice, I noticed the dynamic *immediately after* the final straw. I'd quickly register and acknowledge the many stressors throughout the day that had lead up to that moment. With further regular practice, when an interruption came in the class, I could feel the anger erupting within me—but a small space opened up between the rising emotion and my response to it. I could use this space to tap into the underlying peace that exists within and around all that is. In doing this, I began to identify more with that wider reality than I did with the little me who was feeling frustrated.

With time, I learned to apply this same process to other situations in my life. When my wife was pregnant with our son, for instance, we experienced an emotional dynamic that was difficult for me to handle. My wife, who was a full-time pastor, had many demands on her time and emotional energy, and she was worried about having to shoulder too much of the parenting responsibilities. As the youngest in my family of origin, I had no experience with the demands of young children, but my wife had grown up with a young sister, so she had a better idea what to expect. At the same time, she worried that my past behaviors would mean she would end up having to organize the household while being responsible for the moment-by-moment needs of a young child, that she would have to be the disciplinarian, that my anger would get in the way of my parenting, that I would teach our child to be emotionally distant.

. . . These fear-listing conversations were fueled by her memories of our past issues—but the litany of my all-too-familiar shortcomings triggered my own self-consciousness, anxiety, inadequacy, and withdrawal. My ego felt attacked, and I experienced a profound desire to just escape. No matter what growth I cultivated, some other weakness seemed to always become the new area of focus. I reinforced my wife's fears by being more agitated again at home, while internally, I suffered tension and turmoil. This was a different problem from the one I had faced in the classroom, but I realized I could apply the same practice to it.

With ongoing attentiveness to my reactions, I began to unweave the threads. I acknowledged the emotion moving through me without identifying with it. In the morning, as I sat in contemplation, I invited peace as a foundation for the day ahead. In the evening, when I returned to my time of contemplation, I acknowledged and let go of whatever had transpired during the day.

In both these cases—my frustration in the classroom and my anxiety and withdrawal in reaction to approaching fatherhood—my ego felt threatened. My little self was worried it wouldn't get that to which it felt entitled. My sensitive spots are usually those that connect somehow to my core wound. I want to be well thought of; I want affection and esteem, so the idea of being considered irresponsible, untrustworthy, or inadequate to the fairly commonplace jobs of parenting and teaching grated at my need to feel exceptional. Without consciousness of what was going on, my natural tendency was to identify with a story I told myself about my circumstances. Constant criticism communicated this message to me: "No matter what you do, you'll get no affection or esteem here"—which turned my environment into a fundamental ego threat. Ongoing contemplative practice, however, allowed me to see those emotions well up and to understand the underlying ego structures out of which they came. Practice allowed me to stay rooted in True Self and not to think, feel, and act out unskillfully.

The moment-to-moment task for all of us at this stage of the journey is to observe without judging. To recognize—and let go. As we stay attentive and vigilant to the ways in which the ego wants to latch on to things—to emotions, fears, attachments, insecurities, a victim identity, control, or whatever— we are able to maintain a state of inner balance and equanimity.

This continual release of the ego's demands gives natural joy a chance to well up within us. We become more and more free to detach from our own sense of neediness and instead focus on others. As we increasingly surrender our small self, we find we are empowered to become agents of the Divine.

This won't happen, though, without the ongoing work of *kenosis*—and that work requires a consistent practice that opens up a deepening awareness of the underlying causes of our unskillful responses in thought, emotion, and behavior. This cultivates within us the ability to disidentify with both circumstances and our reactions to them, allowing us to transcend the limitations of the False Self. As Cynthia Bourgeault reminds us in her book *The Wisdom Jesus*, the biblical term for repentance—*metanoia*—may be best translated as "going beyond the mind," "going into greater mind," or "transcending the mind that keeps us trapped in our limited ego-awareness."[4] Without this ceaseless and persistent process, the incessant pull of the ego will drag us under, back down into our anger, our insecurities, and our addictions.

This same dynamic is at play in many modern myths. At the opening of Tolkien's *The Lord of the Rings*, for instance, the death-figure Sauron, having already been defeated long ago, is growing in strength and threatening to return. On the psychological level, we can consider this to be a metaphor for the ego energy within us. We can have profound healing experiences, sudden insight, and genuine growth, but we still have to maintain the diligent practice of inner awareness, of continuous letting go, lest we fall back under the ego's control. This dynamic also affects the quality with which we are able to carry out our vocation. A returning ego can distort and corrupt genuine intention.

But we don't defeat the ego's pull by fighting it directly. That only gives it more energy. As the saying goes, what you resist, persists, and what you accept, changes. On Dante's road, victory is not the result of heroic willpower—which is actually only our ego in disguise—but rather comes through surrendering ego-driven power (just as Tolkien's ring is finally dissolved in the smoldering lava when Frodo and Smeagol let it go).

Sometimes we delude ourselves that we no longer need the daily practice to be the people we want to be. Circumstances, such as moving into a new context, may convince us that we've brought about final and lasting change. Maybe we finally get a new job, or we move to a new community or a new relationship, or we convert to a new faith—and we feel as though we've finally overcome our obstacles to inner maturity. Usually, after a short period, the ego returns and old patterns emerge.

Coming out of the Christian contemplative tradition, Thomas Keating puts it this way:

The heart of Christian ascesis (or discipline) is the struggle with our unconscious motivations. If we do not recognize and confront the hidden influences of the emotional programs for happiness, the False Self will adjust to any new situation in a short time and nothing is really changed. If we enter the service of the Church, the symbols of security, success, and power in the new milieu will soon become the new objects of our desires."[5]

Inner vigilance precedes true outer change. Without an internal process of becoming aware of our unconscious motivations and staying attentive to how they manifest moment to moment, we'll be unable to maintain an others-focused disposition. Our old ego defenses will rise up and claim us yet again.

We must be careful here, however, to distinguish between falling back into unconscious ego patterns and the normal effort required to rise above them. During the beginning of the downward journey or the adoption of some new spiritual discipline such as contemplative practices, our habitual addictions will temporarily increase in intensity. The ego doesn't go quietly but kicking and screaming. Whether we're addicted to drugs or food, sex or applause, achievement or power, the cravings will shoot up as soon as they feel threatened. We have to maintain a disciplined practice and focus in order to weather the storm, accepting the flow of thoughts and emotions, including even our failures and shortcomings. *Acknowledge and let go.*

We also need to keep in mind that the spiritual life goes through cycles. All of us will have fallow periods in which we perceive no new insight and experience no change or breakthrough. Author Carl McColman compares the rhythms of the inner life to those of the body, which experiences wakefulness, fatigue, sleep, dreaming, deep slumber, and awakening again.[6] And yet, as we walk this path, we grow in the capacity for prolonged alert attention. If we don't feel we're experiencing growth, we simply observe and accept it.

In this way, the control the False Self exerts over us will grow less—but it requires constant mindful surveillance of our daily ego processes. At the macro level (our vocations, our affiliations, the communities to which we belong), these may be more obvious, but at the micro level they may fly under our radar if we're not watchful.

Ego processes play out in the details of our day-to-day lives; they show up in our mental chatter, that constant stream of thought we often ignore, endlessly voicing the attention we crave; the ways we pat ourselves on the back or berate ourselves; the small moments of resentment, annoyance, or despair; the deviations from that peaceful center. Eckhart Tolle describes "the incessant streams of involuntary and compulsive thinking" and notes that when we become trapped in these, "the universe really disintegrates for us, and we lose the ability to sense the interconnectedness of all that exists."[7] Teacher Thich Nhat Hanh refers to these tapes in our heads that mediate our daily reality as *mental formations*.[8] To be unconscious is to be completely identified with the mental tapes that play and replay. We confuse them with the self or the "I," when in fact they are conditioned, illusory things.

If fact, in most cases when we say "I," we're not actually talking about the True Self but rather the egoic mind with its thoughts, labels, emotions, and reactive patterns. This egoic mind is a kind of independent entity, but we do not have to identify with it. Doing so, however, is the default state for most of us. So long as that is true, we will continue to experience a distorted reality. We will continue to be asleep. Waking up means achieving a degree of observational distance, so that we can see the ego at work and therefore allow it to dissolve and lose its hold.

But the ego has its ways of maintaining control. It constantly wants to feel distinct, unique, separate, superior. It is never satisfied; it always wants to expand.

This is the mechanism at work behind our complaining, behind our fault-finding, behind our resentments, behind our vilifying, behind anything that knocks us off balance. Our ego attachments, whether things or experiences or relationships we desire or the objects in our lives we think of as "mine," all perpetuate the ego's grasp.

This constructed self also needs to have a conceptual "other" to maintain its sense of separation and control. One way we do this is through a sense of moral superiority. We identify other people's arrogance or materialism, inconsiderate behavior or self-righteousness, and then, by implication, we feel justified in our own moral superiority. The contemplative path allows us to become intimately familiar with our own unconsciousness.

We learn to recognize the ego's many strategies, but we do not judge ourselves when it manifests in unskillful behavior. We simply *see*. As we lift the veil and observe the process at work, it loses its power, sometimes quickly, sometimes gradually.

Weakening the strength of the ego's grip requires a careful attention to observing it in action. Rather than hiding our faults from our own sight, refusing to admit them, we watch our pettiness, our selfishness, our resentment, and our anger at work. We understand their underlying sources. This observation naturally leads to a posture of humility, as we realize our ego processes and mechanisms are just the same as everyone else's. Unconsciousness only varies in degree. That core insight naturally leads to deeper compassion for others as well.

Letting go of our ego attachments allows us to become increasingly aware of our mental-emotional patterns. We understand what triggers us. What we fear. Where our minds go for comfort. We surrender the ego's attempt to shape the world into the form it would have it be, something we usually call the *pursuit of happiness*—which really means changing the conditions around us until they serve our ego's purpose.

The ego may become fixated on the past, unwilling to let it go and move on. Anthony De Mello says that when people go to a counselor for therapy, they don't want to be actually cured.

All they want you to do is to mend their broken toys. "Give me back my wife. Give me back my job. Give me back my money. Give me back my reputation, my success." This is what they want; they want their toys replaced. That's all. Even the best psychologist will tell you that, that people don't really want to be cured. What they want is relief; a cure is painful.[9]

The past can be a place of comfort where we hide—or it can be a set of failures, rejections, and wounds on which we fixate, giving rise to the never-ending tape in our head, the false story we tell ourselves about who we really are.

Some of us, on the other hand, are more future oriented, focusing on a forthcoming state of salvation, whether that's a political utopia, the team winning the championship, or the afterlife in heaven. We live in perpetual state of resignation that our current lives will never be presently fulfilling. Focusing on the future can also provide the illusion of control. If we just consider every possible problem in advance, we believe, we can protect ourselves from suffering. Only it doesn't turn out that way, of course.

These dual directions of the mind, focusing on either the past or the future for fulfillment or pacification, are ongoing distractions. As Eckhart Tolle reminds us, past and present "exist only in the mind as thought forms."[10] They're not real, not here in the *now*.

The cure for this distraction is to fully inhabit the present moment. A complete recognition of the fullness of reality as it is, right now in this very moment, allows us to draw our satisfaction and fulfillment from that level of awareness. Phrases like "living in the moment" and "be here now" have largely become cultural clichés that belie the constant discipline it takes to release our mental fixations on past and present. As sixth-century philosopher and poet Lao Tzu put it, "If you are depressed, you are living in the past. If you are anxious, you are living in the future. If you are at peace, you are living in the present."

We will struggle to be fully present unless we relinquish our habitual tendency to inhabit past, future, or the mental-emotional tapes of some other reality altogether that we make up as we go. Again, the first step is to become *aware*. We notice when we have retreated from the present moment, allowing our ego to dwell in a state of unreality. In keeping focused on *now*, we release our attachments to both the past and the future.

Another form of illusion we human beings often indulge is based on over-identification with groups that help establish our ego project in the world. This group could be our family, our religion, our particular church or denomination, our sports team, our profession, our politics, our nation. These identifications become ego extensions we hide behind. They allow us to profess spiritual maturity and outward humility, since we're no longer focused directly on ourselves, but all we have truly done is to shift our ego project by one degree onto the group with which we identify. We may convince others and ourselves that we have achieved a state of selflessness, giving everything to our place of work, our nonprofit, our school, our church, our family, our country—but if we find our identity in that organization, we will still be trapped, knowing nothing or very little of the internal state of balance, wholeness, and peace. Although we may not display anger and bitterness if someone is unkind to us personally, if someone threatens our group or its labels and values, we react unconsciously and unskillfully with fear, anger, and hostility.

Naturally, no matter how far we travel on our inner journey, we still exist in the social world where groups have meaning and currency. We have a specific language and culture, a nationality, and so on, all of which shape our daily interactions. And unless we retire to a monastery or make some other radical move off the grid, these are still reference points for navigating life. At a higher state of awareness, though, we understand these are only relative terms, provisional and ultimately unreal; we're able to transcend the limited perspective these identifications can impose. We *die* to them. If we don't, to the extent we continue to think in terms of *my* country, *my* status symbol, *my* reputation, *my* political allegiance, *my* consolidated ego-identity whatever it may be, we risk falling back into unconscious dualism, oppositional thinking, and violence. Into resistance. Looking for happiness in a future moment when *my side wins*. And when we cling tightly to the labels with which we identify, our unconscious ego processes will automatically generate an enemy from whom we have to protect *me and mine*.

In day-to-day consciousness, we usually divide the world into roughly three groups: those who help us fulfill our ego projects, or *allies*; those who threaten our ego projects, or *enemies*; and a vast swath of people who do neither, whom, if we are honest, we don't care much about one way or another. If we still identify with our False Self, the ego, as most of us do, we don't really see them, and if we don't see them, we can hardly be capable of loving them. In the highest level of spiritual maturity, however, we are called to love each of these groups, to be receptive and attentive to the ways in which we can work toward wholeness for each of them, day by day and moment by moment. This is not a someday project, to be dreamed about but never achieved; it is an ongoing reality to be *lived*.

The state of present-moment awareness and engagement is always and only right now. This is the only place where we can move beyond the constructed self and get in touch with the radical and transformative love and joy available to the True Self, here in the present moment beneath all conceptualization. In periods of intentional silence, of consciously dwelling in the *now*, the ego and its defenses dissolve and the carefully defined labels melt away. We get a measure of distance. A measure of rest.

This experience of inner expansion and growth isn't necessarily part of a belief system, which at its best is only in service to this awakened and fully present state of being, this deep awareness. As many wisdom teachers and mystics have told us, a thought or a doctrine can *point toward* the truth, but it never *is* the truth. In a similar way, great truths can be put into words, but the words are not the truth itself.

Jesus, using the metaphor of the Kingdom for this state of being, says "the kingdom will not come with observable signs."[11] Instead, the Kingdom to which Jesus referred is a way of seeing, a way of being. It is an ongoing fully awake state, lived in the present moment, of transformation from the inmost self outward. Accurate perception of the truth always requires a mind uncluttered by distorting attachments. Then, as we practice letting go of the vestiges of the False Self in day-to-day practice, we move toward our True Self.

In practice, this True Self is difficult to define. This is in part because it is fluid and dynamic, awake to the shifting realities in which we exist. To describe and label is to fix into place. It is to create another mental category, a concept, a thought form out of which grow further dualisms and division. In contrast, as the author of the Gospel of John writes, "The wind blows where it chooses, and you hear the sound of it, but you do not know where it comes from or where it goes. So it is with everyone who is born of the Spirit"[12]—and so it also is with the True Self.

From the outside, the True Self's behaviors look like forgiveness, patience, peace, lovingkindness, and so on (what the Bible calls the fruits of the Spirit). But the True Self is no namby-pamby pushover; it can also be firm if the situation calls for it. Its external strength comes from our inner experience of simultaneous balance and awareness. As many of the mystics, sages, and wisdom teachers describe, having passed through an experience of refining fire, the death of the False Self, what remains is a kind of pure presence, fearless, deathless. But remember, the True Self is not a thing, not a static identity but truth-in-action. It is love-in-action.

Christ also said, "The kingdom of God is within you."[13] He wasn't speaking to his followers, to the "in-crowd," but to people at a public gathering. In fact, he was responding to the Pharisees, the religious leaders who were among his chief critics. Beneath the layers of ego investment and self-righteousness, even the Pharisees' True Selves have access to the Kingdom. This truth is universal. It is the nature of reality, not a privilege for the elect, for those who "have accepted Christ" and get to go to heaven after they die, as some of us have been taught.

The Divine Kingdom has to do with realizing *who we are* at our most fundamental, elemental level. We can live in the light of that truth, or stay in a state of ignorance and distortion and remain in the dark. Attachment to family, attachment to the past, attachment to possessions are all attachment to a false identity found in external forms. In the Gospels, Jesus conveys a great sense of urgency about helping others to wake up from this illusion.

Unfortunately, we can get stuck at a level of abstraction and never quite sink our teeth into this awareness. Terms like *conscious living, mindfulness,* and *awareness* have become common self-help buzzwords that may be so overused they've been hollowed out of meaning. But remember, each of these words, like all language, is only a sign, something pointing at the reality rather than the reality itself. The actual experience of awareness is quite profound. There's a sense of freedom, expansiveness, and purpose—and a simultaneous sense of both radical independence and generous solidarity with others.

As we keep a vigilant eye on our inner processes, we see our ego against the backdrop of Divine grace. This nonjudgmental self-observation is in fact the seed of grace, which we then naturally extend to others.

When we engage in compulsive thoughts or habitual acting-out behavior, we can now say, "This is happening," rather than, "This is me." Doing this allows the automatic unconscious behavior to gradually dissolve as we become more and more aware of our own mental-emotional egoic patterns. Over time, we approach a state of egolessness.

What does this state of egolessness look like? Eckhart Tolle tells the story of the Japanese Zen teacher Hakuin, a wise man whom people far and wide sought out for wisdom and guidance. When a girl in the village became pregnant, under pressure from her parents she named Hakuin as the father. Confronted with the information, he simply said, "Is that so?" and took loving care of the baby when it was born. His reputation was tarnished, however, and fewer and fewer people came to see him. Later, full of remorse, the daughter confessed that the father was the young man at the butcher shop. Humbled and ashamed, the parents came and asked for the child back. "Is that so?" was all Hakuin said, giving the child back. Tolle comments:

> The Master responds to falsehood and truth, bad news and good news, in exactly the same way. . . . He allows the form of the moment, good or bad, to be as it is. . . . To him there is only this moment, and this

moment is as it is. Events are not personalized. He is nobody's victim. . . . Always responding to what the present moment requires, he lets go. . . .[14]

Most of us have experienced the internalized pain of being defamed. In a state of awareness, we need not identify with this pain; it need not define us. Instead, like Hakuin, we can respond only to what the present moment requires, rather than becoming victimized and handing over power to others to affect our inner state.

For beginners, the obstacles to this state of being are many. One element I struggled with early on in my contemplative practice was the process of emerging from a state of deep peace into everyday situations. The first frustration I experienced after coming out of my time of contemplation would send me into a tailspin of rage. Once, for example, after thirty minutes of sitting is silent awareness, I slowly and mindfully walked into the kitchen of my seminary apartment to make lunch. As I pulled out the silverware drawer, the old wood stuck and I had to yank at it several times to get it open. By the time I did, my peace was shattered, and in my exaggerated anger, I slammed the drawer on the floor.

Other people may experience pangs of anxiety early in their practice, as the unconscious becomes drained like dirty bathwater, leaving the muck at the bottom more visible. In the silence of contemplative practice, images can emerge of times we felt embarrassed, times we failed someone. We can feel the shame or embarrassment from that memory. But the practice asks simply that we acknowledge it without resisting, observe without getting caught up. These thoughts will continue to come, and the practice is to make space for them, to even see them as vehicles for awakening, as they force us to expand and mature enough to make room for them, to accept.

During one period of suffering from a combination of interconnected stressors, this process hit home for me. I had been experiencing an acute sense of guilt and shame about ongoing sexual addiction and acting out, and I seemed to be in constant fights at home, with mounting inner resentment, despite my regular contemplative practice. My young son rarely slept through the night, and my wife and I were frequently on edge and in survival mode. All this seemed very far afield from the stretches of peace I had experienced previously from my contemplative practice. I didn't realize that this was merely another inflection point in my journey until I gained some insight when an old friend recommended the spiritual classic *Awareness* by Anthony De Mello.

The book's simple premise is that all our suffering is caused by our attachment. No one *makes* us happy. No one *makes* us angry. Our underlying attachments are what govern our state of mind and affect our responses when we interact with others. Deep happiness comes only from becoming aware of our attachments and letting them go. Drop the attachment, change the state of mind, change the response.

This articulation helped me comprehend how radical the act of surrender must be, how radical the act of becoming aware of my attachments and cravings as the interconnected bundle of the ego. I don't have to pick up that bundle. I can drop it. True happiness shines through when I've done that. Then I'm free to choose where to respond and how.

For several months after this realization, I felt as though I had super powers. I took radical responsibility for my inner state. I sought out practices to cultivate gratitude first thing in the morning and last thing at night, along with my regular contemplative practice. I experienced a noncontingent happiness for the first time, totally at ease with whatever was the case. Interrupted sleep? Accept it, let go, and be joyful. Criticism from a spouse? Accept it, let go, and be joyful. No time to write this week? Accept it, let go, and be joyful. Lustful thoughts? Accept them, let them go, and be joyful.

Of course this plateau eventually evened out. When it did, lapses in my practice as well as lapses in my peaceful disposition eventually crept back into my life. I'm no sage, no guru. I'm not in a perpetual state of bliss. But I've tasted it. I've drunk from those waters. I've had an experience of awakening, and that gives me hope and resolution for the ongoing journey. I understand, though, that this state of joy is not accidental or coincidental: further dying to myself is necessary, further uncovering, further unmasking before that state can become more and more permanent. My daily contemplative practice constitutes an interruption in this mind-stream, providing a little space of separation between the ego with which I normally identify and a deeper or True Self that is pure awareness.

Over time, as we remain rooted in contemplative practice and teaching, seek out community that supports our practice, and continue in diligent self-observation, we become less and less identified with our False Self or ego. We are able to rest for longer periods in that state of awareness. We become progressively less fixated on recognition, labels, or even the group identities that serve as our ego extensions.

Just as Jesus emptied himself, we, too, can manifest Divinity by entering fully into our humanity, allowing ourselves to be refined and transformed until we can truly let go of the attachments that keep us from the Divinity *that is always already there* within us. That's the paradox of the Incarnation, and it's the profound truth toward which the great mystics and spiritual teachers continuously point us. No one, however, can hand us that truth on a platter. It is not a set of principles. It is not a theology, not a list of concepts to memorize. It's an experience.

We usually only come to this state of awareness through considerable suffering, or what Richard Rohr calls "necessary suffering." In fact, the suffering can be so immense it brings us to a breaking point, a death. This is necessary, Rohr says, because the "false self does not surrender without a fight to its death." He goes on to explain:

> If suffering is "whenever we are not in control" (which is my definition), then you see why some form of suffering is absolutely necessary to teach us how to live beyond the illusion of control and give that control back to God.[15]

For me, suffering came early on in the forms of unmet needs, a fierce desire for things to be a certain way, and fixating on a particular relationship or person as a source of fulfillment and comfort, affection and esteem. I suffered when things turned out quite differently from what I believed they were "supposed to." Much of my inner work had to do with identifying this pattern, and learning to accept the present life situation in general. Later, it wasn't enough to have had insight into the structure and nature of my personal suffering, but instead I had to learn (and still do) how to bring awareness of the eternal present into my daily frustrations and stressors, to observe how these play out and how I tend to respond on the everyday level.

I experience recurring times when desire and attachment create a resistance to the present moment, producing new suffering. During these times, I'm deeply resistant to what is, reluctant to unearth yet a deeper layer of unconscious attachment. I want attention or recognition, peace and quiet or gratification, and in that state of mind, I momentarily see family or my living situation—or even my slow computer—as an obstacle to what I want. In moments of deep presence, I'm fully aware that I can bring peace, acceptance, and an open embrace to that moment, and let go of whatever inner resistance is building. But the challenge is to *do* that, moment by moment.

Yet another challenge is to bring this quality to bear when our foundation is rocked. When we lose the places we go when everything else seems unsafe or uncertain. These sources of comfort and ego support can be a friendship, a role in life, or a belief. We lose them when a relationship breaks, when death comes, when we are laid off or fired, when our children grow up and leave our home, or when doubts and disillusionment set in. Something we thought was fundamental to our very identity is lost. The world seems hostile, alienating.

In fact, this is merely another death to the ego and the world it has constructed. The lesson we learn as we enter more deeply into the emptiness through some form of contemplative practice is that all things in the material world are transient. Everything—every family relationship, every friendship, every role, every achievement—passes away sooner or later (at the very latest when our physical body dies). All gone. The paradox is, however, that this doesn't have to be a source of depression but can instead free us to take delight in the experiences while they're occurring, without the anxiety of impending loss robbing them of their joy. As we let go of our attachments, we inhabit the present moment more fully, without naively clinging to it as a source of ultimate fulfillment. There are many deaths along this path. In going through these deaths, however much necessary suffering they might require, we come to a point of acceptance of *what is*. This allows our inner tapes to quiet, allowing us to see our thought patterns for what they are.

Many of us recognize the ravages of selfishness and feel called to bring greater love into the world—but we may not realize that the biggest obstacle to living in a state of greater love is our own ego with its unconscious desires, needs, and comforts. It is precisely these that we have to confront and surrender at this stage of Dante's road toward wholeness.

And then, as Anthony De Mello puts it, we become as empty and spacious as the sky. And when suffering happens, it's like "when you throw black paint in the air"—there's nothing for it to stick to.[16]

IMAGINE

Looking up from where you sit here at the top of the mountain, you see the vast emptiness of the night sky. Your thoughts drift.

After a moment, you bring your awareness back to your immediate surroundings. Your eyes move from the dancing flames to the infinite expanse of the night sky above. Your face is warmed by the fire, even as the night breeze chills the back of your neck.

You look down at the leather-bound book next to you on the ground. You pick it up, and this time, when you press the tiny latch, it clicks open. You gently open the book and turn to the first worn page.

WAYPOST 8 EXERCISES

Select **at least two or three** exercises:

1. **Residual Shame:** What images do you see in the flame here at the top of the mountain? What residual material still provides you with a sense of fear, embarrassment, or shame? What memories or experiences make you feel small? Write a letter to yourself from an objective perspective. What would you tell yourself about these experiences?

2. **Forgiveness:** Call to mind three of your most painful experiences brought about by another person. Call to mind the person's face. Recall the situation. Feel as vividly as possible the emotion this memory brings up. Prior to naming the feeling as fear or anger or shame, register the physical sensation of the memory in your body. Then speak forgiveness to the person. Take your time with this exercise.

3. **Self-Examination:** Turn a piece of paper into four quadrants. Title the four quadrants Joy, Grief, Hope, and Fear. List as many joys, griefs, hopes, and fears as you can in each quadrant. Then reflect on the areas where you tend to dwell the most and

why. Entering into emptiness and silence can cast a different perspective on our normal mental-emotional patterns.

4. **Sacred Place:** Describe the *place* in your life (the precise location) that you most associate with being at peace in an internal state of harmony. Paint it, draw it, write a poem about it, make a collage about it, write a song about it, or simply describe the experience of being there. Try to capture the effect it has on you.

5. **Permission:** What activity in your life allows you to immerse yourself fully, when you forget yourself for a time and are one with the act you're performing? Commit to doing that activity for at least one hour this week.

6. **Visio Divina:** Take a close look at the paintings of Chinese painters Shi Lu, Chang Dai-Chien, and Zhang Daqian. What might the connection be between this style of painting and *kenosis*, the experience of emptying your identity of self?

7. **Audio Divina:** Listen to a song that invokes letting go and new perspectives for you. (My selections:

"With God on Our Side" by Bob Dylan, "Washing of the Water" by Peter Gabriel, and "A Sense of Wonder" by Van Morrison.)

8. **Poetica Divina:** Read the poems "April Inventory" by W. D. Snodgrass, "God, Whose Love and Joy" by Angelus Silesius, and "Zazen on Ching-t'ing Mountain" by Li Po. What resonates most with you from these works?

9. **Lectio Divina:** Philippians 2:5–11 (Read, Reflect, Respond, *Rest*).

NOTES

1. Taken from Psalm 51: "You will sprinkle me with hyssop and I shall be cleansed. You will wash me, and I will be whiter than snow" (*A New English Translation of the Septuagint* by Albert Pietersma and Benjamin G. Wright, Oxford University Press, 2007).

2. According to Abe Masao in his essay "Kenotic God and Dynamic Shunyata," in *The Emptying God: A Buddhist-Jewish-Christian Conversation* (Maryknoll, NY: Orbis Books, 1990), *shunyata* "is a dynamic and creative function of emptying everything and making alive everything." He explains that like *kenosis, shunyata* is not a one-time event but must be practiced day to day in every moment and in every action.

"True shunyata is not *shunyata* thought by us, but *shunyata* lived by us."

3. Philippians 2:6–9, The Berean Bible.

4. Cynthia Bourgeault. *The Wisdom Jesus* (Boulder, CO: Shambhala, 2013).

5. Thomas Keating. *Invitation to Love: The Way of Christian Contemplation* (Rockport, MA: Element, 1992), pages 14–15.

6. Carl McColman.. *Answering the Contemplative Call: First Steps on the Mystical Path* (Newburyport, MA: Hampton Roads, 2013).

7. Eckhart Tolle. *A New Earth: Awakening to Your Life's Purpose* (New York: Penguin, 2008), page 276.

8. Thich Nhat Hanh points out that mental formations can be positive as well as negative, and we can learn to replace the negative formations with the positive. He writes: "In my tradition of Buddhism we learned that there are fifty-one categories of mental formations—you fear, your despair, your love, your compassion, your mindfulness. Mindfulness is one of the fifty-one categories of mental formations. . . . That is good news, because if you know how to practice every day, then mindfulness can be generated as an energy, to do the work of recognizing, embracing, transforming and healing." ("Taking Care of Our Mental Formations and Perceptions," Dharma Talk given on August 3, 1998, in Plum Village, France; https://www.dhammatalks.net/Books2/Thich_Nhat_Hanh_Taking_Care_of_Mental_Formations_and_Perceptions.htm)

9. Anthony De Mello. *The Spiritual Wisdom of Anthony de Mello* (Altenmunster, Germany: Jazzybee Verlag, 2012).

10. Eckhart Tolle. *A New Earth*, page 130.

11. Luke 17:20, Berean Study Bible.

12. John 3:8, NRSV.

13. Luke 17:21, KJV.

14. Eckhart Tolle. *A New Earth*, pages 199–200.

15. Richard Rohr. *Eager to Love: The Alternative Way of Francis of Assisi* (London: Hodder & Stoughton, 2005), page 26.

16. Anthony De Mello. *The Spiritual Wisdom of Anthony de Mello*, page 61.

Love is the greatest power in the universe. Love is the dynamic center of life, the energy that is at the very core of creation. The mystic uses the energy of love to make the greatest of journeys: the journey of the soul back to the source, the lover back into the arms of the Beloved. The power of love transforms the seeker, revealing within the heart the secret of oneness, the mystical truth that lies beyond the veils of duality: "All is One."

–LLEWELLYN VAUGHAN-LEE

Love is blind? No, attraction is blind. There is nothing in the world so clear sighted as love.

–ANTHONY DE MELLO

Into Love

Waypost 9

When he reaches the outer limits of Paradise, the sphere of the fixed stars, three of the biblical saints—Peter, James, and John—confront Dante. He has to pass a test from each of them before he can move on to the angelic *Primum Mobile* (the outermost sphere of the universe) that gives motion to all the other spheres, and then finally into the *Empyrean*, the realm of God beyond all concepts.

First, Dante has to prove himself worthy of this Divine vision by demonstrating an understanding of the three heavenly graces. Once Dante successfully passes St. Peter's test of true faith and St. James's test of true hope, the light of this sphere becomes so brilliant that Beatrice dare not smile and reflect any more of God's radiance to Dante, lest he be turned into a pile of ash. The human mind and body can handle only so much intensity.

When Dante turns to Beatrice, he finds that he can't see her at all anymore. He's gone blind. Now it's St. John turn to stand before him and ask him of his central aim or purpose. Dante answers: "To direct my love toward God." He explains that though we are born with distorted love, we learn to bring that love into alignment with the Divine will, to love what is good. Existence itself is an act of love. Christ's sacrifice was an act of love. All creation turns the heart toward God in love. As soon as he finishes his answer, the souls around him sing out as one: "Holy, holy, holy!" confirming his answer.

Now when Dante turns back to Beatrice, the rays from her eyes remove the chaff from his. He's able to see again but much more clearly than ever before. With his new vision, he looks back down to Earth far below, and he sees with clarity and detail what is happening there. Then he turns his gaze upward and sees souls ascending, drifting like snowflakes in reverse, toward the highest heavenly realms. Finally, when he looks at Beatrice, her beauty grows yet again, and the two are transported into the next heavenly sphere. He has passed his test.

IMAGINE

As you sit beside the fire, the leather-bound book open in your lap, you read by the flames' flicker the first inscription on its weathered pages:

> To come to the land of love,
> we have to pass through the pains of death,
> for to love persons is
> to have died to the need for persons
> and to be utterly alone.

These words, taken from Anthony De Mello,[1] seem a strange way to articulate the reality of love. To enter the land of love we have to *die*, to be *utterly alone*? Isn't love inherently relational?

We tend to think of love as a feeling, as a strong attachment to something. Or we might think of it as a universal need. We might assume it is the affection or feelings we have for others that manifests in how we treat them. If we think in more theological terms, calling to mind the *agape*-love of the New Testament, we may see love as a freely given, transformational gift. But in all these cases, we are thinking of love in personal terms. At this stage of the journey, however, we are invited to have our understanding of the nature and reality of love expanded.

Dante's road has led us to love's paradox. Love is both intimate and impersonal. It is both comforting and shattering. It integrates our faults, but also keeps us in utter humility before the Divine. We experience love as Divine therapy, moving us toward a greater wholeness, but we also encounter love as an elemental force, a preexisting energy to which our inmost being is mysteriously connected.

We can become more and more open to love, more and more aware of it, and increase our ability to manifest it in the world. The great mystics teach of a capacity to *dwell in love*, to channel love, of love-in-action moment to moment. Arriving at a place on our journey where we are able to dwell in love is one understanding of coming home. This elemental love is not something we find outside ourselves but is instead an aspect of our inmost essence that grows as we let go of our illusory attachments and the search for ego gratification.

In this chapter we want to understand this process of refinement and movement that leads to love as the utter awareness of the Divine nature, regardless of changing circumstances. The mystics teach of love as both the essential component out of which creation itself was fashioned and a quality of being to which ultimately we can only open ourselves by the intentional practice and ongoing disposition of emptiness and dying to self. Divine love is source, goal, and process of the total transformation of the self.

In letting go of what we think we are and what the False Self clings to for survival and comfort, we open ourselves to Divine love—and yet paradoxically, part of what the ego clings to for comfort and survival is precisely what we traditionally think of as our love relationships in family, in partnerships, in community. The challenge of Divine love is the shattering of all our dependencies that keep us from love's full flowering within us.

I had to learn this for myself experientially, despite having grown up in a warm and loving family. One of my mom's great gifts was to build a hospitable atmosphere, to give care, with meals, with music, with keeping a household diligently, sacrificially. Meanwhile, my dad found his greatest pride in his three sons. Fundamentally, the home was supportive and affectionate. But from an egoic perspective, there is something obligatory about familial love, something dutiful that sets limits on its value as a source of fulfillment and affirmation. Family is *supposed* to love you.

Over the years, I have learned from the lives of close friends how difficult life can be when that foundational love is missing, but growing up, I took it for granted. To my mind a love that conferred value was that which was freely chosen and freely given. I was taught in church that Christ had chosen to love me and this love was freely on offer, and yet it always seemed a little abstract—and there was also the threat of hellfire and damnation if I chose not to accept Christ, so this love also felt forced and obligatory. The only unforced options left were friendship, and more important and more intense, romantic love. To my mind, this type of love, since it's not forced upon anyone, was the one that mattered most. A partner is under no obligation to love you.

This singular focus on romantic relationships as the true measure of value and source of validation was so prevalent in me from such an early age that I can't remember a time when I didn't think in these terms. As I grew older, this placed an incredible amount of pressure on my romantic relationships, especially early on. I had expectations that were far beyond any hope of being met.

For most of us, the first stage of love tends to be egocentric: we're looking for validation, especially outside the family system. My first young relationship began innocently and casually enough, but I soon invested in the relationship with reckless abandon all my hope of fulfillment. What else could possibly matter? Someone had freely chosen to be with me.

But few teenagers are ready for a lifetime commitment, and when my girlfriend revealed she had slept with another guy, I was devastated. The entanglements of adolescent sexuality, which had been a kind of distant abstraction, a remote desire up to that point, became a painful present. The fallout was immediate. I not only felt rejected by my girlfriend but also ashamed and embarrassed among my friends. I believed my girlfriend must see me as inadequate and immature.

After that, I was cautious about investing too much into a relationship, despite my intense and singular desire to have that particular need met. Most of my relationships were short-lived. Later, I fell in love with someone at an International School, in part, I think now, because she was from another country and only visiting for a short time. She was familiar but exotic, alive, creative, witty, passionate, and unself-conscious—and a long-distance relationship felt intrinsically safer. There was no risk of local embarrassment if something went wrong. The drama of other people's input and opinions didn't matter. This relationship could be a separate little cocoon, pure, untainted, influenced only by the quality and intensity of love we brought to it in phone calls and in letters. Furthermore, there was a pathos and piquancy to the role of long-suffering lovers kept apart by circumstance, time, and geography.

After graduation, I visited Australia, where my girlfriend lived, and spent a month with her family before returning to America. A classmate also came to visit during the tail end of my trip, and the three of us spent a couple days sightseeing. Meanwhile, I had been looking into attending college in Australia, while my girlfriend investigated performing arts programs in the United States. We talked as if marriage was inevitable. And then, a few months later, as I was sitting with a group of friends, the classmate who had visited us in Australia bragged about sleeping with my girlfriend. At first I thought he was joking, but then the realization set in: he wasn't kidding. As shame and humiliation spread through my body like toxin, I fought the urge to indulge in a violent outburst.

The relationship with my Australian girlfriend never truly recovered. After it gradually faded, a kind of resignation set in that this seemingly intrinsic, fundamental need I had would never be fulfilled. I was convinced that any relationship that seemed to offer me what I craved so much would inevitably lead to an even deeper pain of loss and humiliation.

In later dating relationships, I kept a degree of emotional distance, or I would only enter if the water seemed absolutely safe. My next significant relationship was with someone with many attractive qualities—she was beautiful, kind, courteous, and always looking for the best in other people—but I maintained a high degree of control, never fully trusting her enough to be vulnerable. This was also another long-distance relationship—she lived in Germany, while I was in college in the United States—that required neither time from my daily life nor the ordinary compromises necessary to all relationships when two people are seeing each other regularly. Instead, all our interactions carried a deep emotional intensity, without the hard work that would have been required in a different sort of relationship. The fact that she was a good deal younger than me and deferred to me in many ways made me feel that much more comfortable.

When she moved to London for medical school, however, that changed, and I experienced intense anxiety. I could not imagine how I would fit into her future life; I had no picture of where she was currently spending her time or with whom. She'd find more likeminded people in her med program, I was certain. The big city would expand her horizons, she would realize our relationship wasn't as special as she had thought, and she would inevitably decide she could do better. Rather than suffer another painful humiliation, I broke off the relationship before she could.

Even after we had broken up, though, she remained a kind of Beatrice figure for me, a symbol of the impossible love for which I longed. I'd quietly invoke her name when the world seemed too cold or alien or corrosive, or if I became too self-conscious. Her name served as a talisman or incantation to invoke the qualities of gentleness, acceptance, beauty, warmth, and loving-kindness I'd felt from her; her memory was a kind of security blanket against the cold. Psychologically, she was my home base, conveying to me the greater sense of at-home-ness I'd experienced during the times we were together during my summer and winter breaks, when I returned to my family's home in Germany. The relationship with her had combined with a sense of place, of rest and recognition, of foundation with family and close friends, and at the same time was free from the daily grind and responsibilities of graduate studies or work. Now, at this stage of my life, she came to represent that earlier period of support and love. By extension, her memory combined for me an entire bundle of loves: brotherly and familial, as well as romantic.

We stayed in close contact over the years and even planned a summer trip to the Mediterranean once I finished my master's program. Then, for a couple weeks during the winter before the planned trip I wasn't able to get in contact with her. During this period I visited my parents in their new assignment in Oregon. When a newborn baby died in their congregation, I attended the memorial service and sat with the family and community honoring this death in their lives. Afterward, I reached out to process the experience with my ex-girlfriend. Again she wasn't available.

I assumed she must have finally cut the cord and moved on, and at the same time, I remembered that she had always said she didn't want children. I knew I did, and something in the atmosphere of grief surrounding this newborn's death had me questioning the value of continuing to invest in a relationship divided over such a central issue. Becoming a caretaker of new life felt sacred, precious; and sharing a community's grief as it mourned this child somehow confirmed that feeling for me. I realized that after years of holding onto this connection with my ex-girlfriend, it was time to honor it, grieve its passing, and let it go. If I didn't, I would be trapped in the past, unable to grow.

In each of these romantic relationships, despite their intensity and sense of intimacy, there was also an immature quality. The ideal relationship for me was an escape, a cocoon, a return to the womb, where I could be solitary, safe, uninfluenced by the outside world. Author Ken Wilber writes that this kind of love is typical of the egocentric stage of development, and he describes the reality he had to experience in his own life as he slowly learned "that love did not mean holding on," as he had always thought, "but rather letting go."[2]

Egocentric love is a desire for connection and validation in the external world for ourselves alone. In my life, this meant that my only goal in romantic relationships was to have my own inner needs met. On the surface I might be passionate, caring, and giving, but beneath the surface I did not want any kind of love that required growth, change, or compromise. This was a kind of hoarding or acquisitive love. The mythical image for this is the dragon sitting atop his treasure hoard. It's love as possession. It's an exchange that says, "I'll love and care for you *provided that* you continue to make me feel good about myself."

I was unaware of my soul's true needs. As Llewellyn Vaughan-Lee writes,

> The spiritual wayfarer is seeking a deeper fulfillment than even the most loving human relationship can offer. How often is this need projected onto human relationship, a relationship which is limited by the very fact that it is human?[3]

The ensuing years of deep frustration stemmed in part from my inability to recognize the real source of what I longed for. I was unable to find a love relationship that felt connective, familiar, to find a *home*, but I was looking in the wrong place.

Meanwhile, other areas of my life proved to be just as disappointing. In faith communities, I often found myself on the margins, never quite comfortable but unsure about any kind of alternative for spiritual community. I took a job that often felt like an endless uphill battle. I was lost—and longing to go home.

Then I met someone with a shared sense of humor and a similar view on life. During the dating stage of our relationship, it did feel like home. This woman was confident, energetic, and fiercely loyal, with a magnetic personality, but she also carried a wisdom brought about by personal suffering. We had both led nomadic lives and respected each other's experience, integrity, and values. We bonded over an appreciation for Wendell Berry, and we were talking about marriage after only a couple months.

We did marry, but as is common in many marriages, the first year was fraught with challenges and differing expectations. Uncomfortable roles, loss of outside relationships, hectic schedules, and tight finances all contributed to a sense of inner tension and dissatisfaction. As I fought battles on multiple fronts every day, I had no sense at all of *home*. I became mentally fixated on past relationships and the sense of intensity, care, and support I'd felt in them. My marriage and life situation at the time felt like a barrier cutting me off from all those things I had come to rely on for a sense of home.

Of course no single relationship can realistically carry the burden of meeting all our needs for security and fulfillment. It wasn't until I began to see the effect of my own disposition and intention on the world around me that changes began to occur. Until then, I had a sense of passivity, as though things over which I had no control had led me to this impasse, to a life situation that was unsupportive and overly demanding.

The daily practice of Centering Prayer gave me a sense of agency. As I dove more deeply into a contemplative practice, I began to be more aware of my own inner dynamics, the resentments and their sources. As I have already described, I developed a sense of the self or "me" on the one hand that is acting and reacting, thinking and evaluating, feeling and needing, extending and withdrawing, and another self or an "I" from some timeless place that is simply observing, watching, noticing, attending. One is what teacher Roger Castillo calls "the doer who expects outcomes" and the other is "the witnessing presence." I began to be able to act lovingly even when not feeling loved.

This aspect of the self, the witness or observer, is aware of choice in reaction, aware of the way patterns of thought and emotion create the perception of the world around us. I began to realize that the yearning I felt for home couldn't be met by family, by a Christian community, by my job, by relationships or marriage, or by any other pursuit.

For me, a sense of inner choice and agency began to grow from this little space of awareness. Over time, I could choose not be stuck in a reactive mode where I felt a physical pain like a cannonball in the gut, believing that none of my deepest needs for connection were likely to be fulfilled in this life. I was still a bundle of insecurities, sensitivities, and addictions, but with daily contemplative practice, a quiet space opened up within me, a neutral space of simple, nonjudgmental observation. This created in me a gentleness where there had been firmness and resistance. Gratitude where there had been resentment. A sense of attunement with a larger reality. I began to bring *intentionality* to my environment.

I had been brought up to bless others, to only speak kindness, to watch my tongue; I was also taught that God knew my every thought, and so I should be very watchful of even my thoughts, lest they be displeasing. Without the inner development to go along with those beliefs, they became an untenable form of rigid control, a spirituality of perfection. I tended to pull in the opposite direction from such beliefs, away from perpetual self-denial toward sensory pleasure and indulgence. But now that I was developing an inner awareness, I could see the positive value in finding ways to speak a genuine kindness or to bring a gentle word, to encourage someone on a difficult day, or to just find a moment to make sure my students know they were noticed and supported.

I had relocated the source of my sense of self. My mood and joy were no longer dependent on my wife's mood or attention or fatigue level when she came home from work. As I displaced an egocentric way of being with a more *other*-centric, I became much less self-conscious, and I looked for small ways to make other people's day better. Naturally, this change did not happen immediately or even quickly; prolonged periods of withdrawn stewing in self-centered thinking still overcame me—but nevertheless, my center of gravity had shifted significantly, leaving far more room for others in my field of vision.

Given my own longstanding addictions, I joined a twelve-step group for accountability and fearless honesty, where I could sit in a state of illuminated truth, sharing and listening, trusting and revealing. In doing so, I was able to listen to others and make a space for their stories. This receptivity and experience of simple, honest community was a form of love. Serving in this space deepened that love.

Soon, I was able to take delight in simple things I hadn't felt in years. The world seemed to open up again, and I felt gratitude for colors, for changes in light. I enjoyed flavors and sounds with greater intensity. I could celebrate the successes of others and genuinely wish them well, rather than secretly wishing their success had been mine. An inner constriction slackened, and I became open to life again.

This inner change paved the way for Divine grace to enter my external life as well. Only days after I attended my first twelve-step gathering, my wife called with the news that she was pregnant. It was like God saying, *Okay, you've learned something about love, about surrender, so now you're ready. Here you go.*

During that period in our lives, my wife was serving as an associate pastor at a Presbyterian church in San Diego. At the same time that my capacity for joy and gratitude were growing, we were showered with care from a community where I had been little more than a stranger. People left meals on our doorstep anonymously. Doctors in the church offered free services when my wife suffered from headaches. After the baby was born, younger students in the church volunteered to babysit. Others helped out on occasion as night nannies so we could catch up on our sleep. People warmly embraced us before, during, and after services, and then they sent us home with blankets and onesies, snacks and books.

I also saw my wife and the church demonstrate caring for the extended community and the broader world, organizing services to Haiti after the devastating earthquake there and helping orphanages for disabled children in Mexico through building projects and free medical clinics. I was soon asked to lend my own services in small ways, teaching a Lenten poetry series here, running a spiritual formation workshop there. When the music director for one of the services moved on, I was asked to play music. After opening up internally, I found I was now included in an economy of grace through an extended community.

The opening that takes place at this stage of the journey has great beauty. We understand we are part of something greater than ourselves. Committing to acts of service and giving comes more readily and naturally. We become rooted in love and an authentic desire to see others move toward a greater wholeness. Genuine service to others moves us further out of the stories in our head; it puts our own problems in perspective, helps break down walls, and connects us to other individuals and communities. It brings healing, both within and without. This is the agape-love of the New Testament, a love that seeks no reward.

But even in genuine service, ego and attachments—the desire to be recognized for one's efforts or to be validated by an authority figure—can creep back into our minds. We can develop a sense of guilt for not giving enough, or a sense of resentment and burnout when we feel we've given too much. This compassion fatigue is common in caring professions like teaching, social work, healthcare, and the pastorate. As a result, service is most effective and enduring when rooted in a greater love that extends beyond our individual selves. In agape, there is an alignment between the grace and transformation we receive and our actions in the world, a natural cycle similar to breathing. In the Christian tradition, Christ is the ultimate manifestation of this spiritual love.

As we have explored throughout the previous chapters, the process of refinement, purgation, and illumination is necessary to bring us to this place of grace and love. The profound confrontation with the ego and the relinquishing of any and all attachment make the inflow and outflow of love possible. In the teachings of the great mystics, this is the devastating aspect of love. It demands a burning and a death—and yet it is also the animating force of an abundant, eternal life. Its aim is wholeness, which involves the shattering of the illusions that keep us from completion and integrity. Furthermore, this state of health and unity is never purely individual. It goes beyond personal development and self-actualization.

The mystics suggest there is a love beyond theological categories, beyond reason and concept, beyond both agape and eros. This love is an elemental force that transforms by stripping away. Its goal is a total surrender to Divine truth, to Ultimate Reality, beyond the limits of the separate self we think we are with its comforts and desires, its attachments to wealth, to belongings, to family, to identity, to reputation, to a name, to thoughts, to body.

In this ultimate sense, love is not something we either have or don't have. That idea is merely a story we tell ourselves. Ultimate love simply *is*, abundantly available beneath the surface dross. It's what remains when the ego has been surrendered, when our sense of a self has burst like a bubble. We can distract ourselves with the contrived dramas of the mind—or we can learn to open ourselves, daily, continuously, to this ever-present, ever-available reality. When the veils are torn away and we see no longer through a glass darkly, but face to face,[4] what remains is not a self as we conventionally understand it but only love.

This is the love that brings us to the end of ourselves and beyond. It is what first drew us on our inner journey, following Dante's path of radical transformation that upends our fundamental notions of reality. It brings us to the Dark Night of the Soul[5] and demands that we acknowledge our absolute poverty of spirit. Our egos begin to dissolve into dust, as all desire, all attachment, all craving, all unconscious motivation, all the layers of the illusory self become visible in love's light. This experience may involve our emotions, but it is not contingent upon any emotion.

The process of purgation can be harrowing, but it is also life-giving. In it we die; through it we are born again. Retroactively, all things that have brought us to this point are redeemed or seen in their right perspective. We look in a new way at our earnest search for love and the disappointments that fray at the ego. Everything we experienced that stripped away our illusions becomes both painful and graceful. We come to recognize love as a rain that falls on the just and the unjust alike,[6] as a sun the gives light to everything, as a flower whose fragrance is freely given. It is generous, indiscriminate, fundamental.

This unfurling of our understanding of reality is an inflection point on the soul's journey home. It's part of the pattern we see in the biographies of the great mystics and even in the life of Christ himself. In the Gospels, before Jesus begins his ministry, he enters the wilderness, where he retreats into a deep solitude, a lonely confrontation with his core needs, his ego attachments and desires—and then he releases them. He emerges from this period with the ability to manifest an absolute love, immune to social conventions, praise, or blame. Similar experiences hold true for many other mystics and contemplatives who have a cave or wilderness experience, leaving society and relationship to engage in a deeply internal confrontation. Passing through an inner death, they emerge transformed, able to extend the love they now bear to the farthest reaches, no longer dependent on reciprocity or their own need. Whether we look at the life and writings of Ignatius of Loyola, Francis of Assisi, or Teresa of Avila, this pattern of inner death followed by expansive love holds true. Dionysius the Areopagite, a fifth-century mystic, also described this process, writing that the first step to manifesting real love is purification.[7]

To get a better picture of this kind of love, imagine that the self-giving love we have for our children extends to all creation. This is probably the closest we can come to comprehending what it means to see through the Divine eye. This love comes from a transcendent source, or in the Christian tradition, from God. Love isn't something we achieve or obtain, but rather what remains—what was already there—when falsehood and illusion fall away. Jesuit Anthony De Mello recounts a Chinese saying: "When the eye is unobstructed, the result is sight. When the ear is unobstructed, the result is hearing. When the heart is unobstructed, the result is love."[8]

The process of refinement as our illusions drop away requires *being alone*. Although we may first achieve this state in physical solitude, a spiritual and psychological aloneness is what's really required. The False Self needs others to prop itself up, to give it energy to feed on, and in our default state, the sense of being alone can be torture. This is precisely the part of us that needs to die in order to realize this greater love—but it does not go willingly. In solitude, however, the True Self is filled with an ever-present love. Being alone means we've dropped the need for others, the conventions of causes and groups, of national or family identity. These labels are no longer primary to our essential being. We can enjoy them when they are healthy and balanced, and we can connect and contribute where appropriate—but they no longer affect us at the level of our inmost being, which is eternal.

The very creation in which we exist partakes of love, if only we have the eyes to see. Paradoxically, we realize that even in physical solitude, as Christ was in the wilderness, we are never truly alone, for love is with us.[9] In withdrawing from our need for approval, affection, and power, we become firmly rooted in the ever-flowing grace that is beyond concepts and beyond striving. We transcend our inner wounds, and now, severed from emotional and psychological need, we are free to love. Love pours forth from us.

For me, the keys to experiencing and dwelling in this kind of love has been a combination of my ongoing practice, regular immersion in contemplative teaching, and community. All three are important for my development. At this stage of my journey, my capacity to love others indiscriminately, to dwell in and radiate love directly, corresponds with my diligence in these three areas. It's like medicine: if I take it regularly and in sufficient doses, it cures me of the False Self that obstructs my capacity to dwell in love and act in love. As I continue on this never-ending journey, I experience breakthroughs, periods of prolonged depth and awareness, and also, of course, periods of returning unconsciousness and ego dominance. After a gradual relinquishing may come renewed inner tension, that builds to a release and a new level of openness and being.

Love's practice involves this ongoing inner excavation. It happens sometimes in intense moments of concentrated surrender, but also through a steady and ongoing awareness throughout the day of our own resentments, vindictiveness, and pettiness as they arise, combined with the commitment to examine the sources of these feelings. This attentive, nonjudgmental observation of our inner dynamics changes our relationship with ourselves and our relationship with others. Our own processes and patterns become part of our perceptual field, as much as a car or a tree or a building might be to the physical eye. They are something *there* but the more we observe them, the less we identify with them as us. A daily contemplative practice also helps to usher in the awareness that the entire human drama is playing out against the backdrop of Divine grace. Life is saturated with that grace.

Attending to the body and our physical dynamics helps us maintain a state more conducive to the process of contemplative transformation. This is part of the total transformation into wholeness. The mystic paradoxically seeks the annihilation of the self in order to find wholeness in relationship to others, to the natural world, to daily work, and to what is consumed, both physically and mentally. We care for the body and the mind, while at the same time seeking an unbroken relationship with God.

The process of Divine transformation allows us to recognize that ultimately, we are far more than our emotions, our physical condition, or our external surroundings. Although we are in the process of transformation, strangely, we are becoming what we *already are*. The mystic drops the inner attachments and false perspectives that obstruct the realization of the reality that we are already whole.

As we continue along this path, we find that in a deep sense all the conditions for happiness are already there in our lives. If we set aside the provisional clinging ego and its needs for a moment, then we can ask ourselves: *What do we need to add? What needs to be accomplished? Whose approval matters? What is incomplete? What is worth the sacrifice of peace?* The answers are: *Nothing.* Arriving at this kind of absolute freedom is both death and Divine gift. We relocate the source of happiness from these temporal, changing relationships, which cause both anxiety and need, to the eternal loving presence of God. Happiness can now become noncontingent. Love can become unconditional. We can move into a space of peace *that passeth all understanding.*[10] The alternative is to be stuck on a hamster wheel, chasing temporary ego gratification.

On the contemplative path, we recognize the distinction between the spiritual plane (the Unmanifested, the *tehom*,[11] that empty place of fullness and potentiality out of which creation itself is formed) and the manifested world (the phenomenal world, the created order with its contingencies and relationships, its apparent subjects and objects). Even as we grow in our contemplative practice to the extent we can taste of the Unmanifested, we are still incarnate beings. This is one of the paradoxes at the heart of the mystical path. We are both timeless and in time. Within an underlying unity exist an apparent multiplicity of forms. The two are mysteriously connected.

Part of the task of contemplative practice is to become more and more aware of this dynamic. After engaging in this process for many years, I have realized that so many of the debilitating, anxiety-producing situations I experience come back to losing this awareness. My ego suffers if I let someone down, because I hate being perceived as unreliable, irresponsible, or disappointing— as if creating a good impression was the highest goal in life, rather than loving-kindness or commitment or diligence or peace. *Seeming admirable* has often meant more to me than *being*. From daily small-scale anxieties to large scale addictions and acting out, I have learned to see that the threads connect back to the same shadow or False Self, the same egoic desires.

The awareness that these desire are both real and unreal comes when we observe them like shadows in our consciousness, naming them, admitting them, sharing them. As we no longer play cover-up games, Divine love, both ever-present and preexistent, can begin to flow through us more strongly. In my own life, I have learned that my deep need for approval from people I love is an obstacle to the flow of this greater love. Severing these ties internally has been a path from needy love to a radiant love that is not self-seeking.

To reinforce this awareness, I engaged in a mental practice of calling to mind all the significant people in my life—however tender, however warm, however loving—and then claiming emphatically: *I do not need you for me to be happy. I do not need your approval for me to be happy. I do not need your affection for me to be happy.* Paradoxically, this inner separation from ego-fulfilling dependencies empowered me to give attention, energy, focus, and love to people I wouldn't have even seen before. Being severed from the self-centered need for affection and approval enabled me to be a loving presence in others' lives in more mature ways.

This mental cord-cutting allowed me to see my relationships in fresh ways. I could choose what to bring to the table, decide if an uncomfortable truth needed to be spoken—or not. As I became far less concerned with confining myself to an acceptable version of myself for others' validation, I experienced greater freedom of self-expression. I was able to maintain my peace regardless of others' approval or disapproval.

Today, my affection for friends and family is as great as ever, but I'm not dependent on them for my sense of well-being, which now is independent, noncontingent. I understand that others have their own perspectives, hang-ups, and egoic needs, and dancing to each of these tunes would be tiresome and fruitless. Beneath all of these transient relational dynamics lies a deeper reality, and my contemplative practice cultivates a hunger for the timeless essence that can be veiled by the surface play of the ego-mind.

Although relationships may be good in and of themselves, we may need to cut the cord to our sources of stability and comfort, including our marriage relationship, our images of our friends or children, and even our image of God. When we remove the default picture, we make space for a newer, truer, less ego-filled image to emerge. With the phrase "dying before you die," the mystics imply that by drawing this practice into every area of life, we enter the darkness of love that while it burns away also incubates and transforms. As we enter into the silence behind the words, the darkness behind the images, we discover a greater fullness, a wider reality.

Going ever deeper on this spiritual path, our understanding of love continues to expand. While we begin with a desire for love as an ego support mechanism, filtered through the lens of our own particular desires and hang-ups, we widen that notion to encompass a broader set of relationships of care and support, of peacemaking, justice, and service. With Dante, we encounter a deeper teaching, according to which love unlocks and releases the very notion of a self.

Reality holds a vast elemental love to which we are mostly blind, our vision blocked by our mind-made obstacles, our contrived dramas, our neediness, our persistent ego that finds fault or clings to problems, that lives in an idealized past or fears a horrific future. William Blake called these mental constructs our "mind-forg'd manacles." But as the sense of self loosens, love becomes a quality we exude rather than something we feel we have or don't have. In the process of inner transformation, on the journey home, love integrates even our wounds, even our addictions, into the process of becoming whole.

IMAGINE

Here at the top of the mountain, by the silver light of the wheeling stars, you read the book the cowled stranger gave you. It tells you of pathways to love. You read about mystics and contemplatives, deep pain and Divine healing.

The book explains ancient practices that will open you to the process of purgation, illumination, and union.

You pause in your reading and look up from the page, realizing that there is nothing to stop you from beginning these practices now, in this very moment. You start by simply quieting your mind, paying attention to the thoughts that come, and then releasing them. You allow them to simply drift away without getting caught up in their siren song.

Memories come, of the darkness of the cave, the fear at the bottom, the abbey, the forest, a merchant, the climb up the mountain, the three strangers. With each thought that comes, you notice it, acknowledge it, recognize the degree of emotional response that accompanies it, and then release it. A distant rustle in the grass momentarily distracts you, but you simply recognize the distraction, release it, and return to the silence. A few moments later, you notice physical sensations—an itch, a twinge of your muscles, a momentary discomfort in your belly. You recognize these distractions and then release them as well.

An inner quiet grows like a substance unto itself. In this space there is no thought, no name, no disappointment, no approval, no disapproval, no action or reaction. Simply peace. A peace in which all striving dissolves. A peace tinged with the qualities of joy and love. A peace beyond understanding. A causeless joy. An objectless love that radiates outward.

After a time, you return your attention to the physical space around you—the dead leaves and moss on the ground, the night sky, the breeze, the fire's warmth and light and crackle. As you gaze into the flames, you again see a vision there. This time you see the faces of grandparents and feel the gentle warmth of their inner essence, as if they were there with you. You feel the presence of a loving parent. You see the room in which you felt most at home when you were young. The faces of siblings and close friends from childhood, from adolescence, from adulthood, all smile at you, and you feel the energy of their presence. Next, you look into the eyes of coworkers, colleagues, and people in your various communities; you return their smiles. You sense the presence of beloved partners and children, and you call to mind times of loving connection, occasions when you gladly sacrificed for them, when they showed loving appreciation. You see the faces of those you've served well, those to whom you've given yourself, and you experience the warmth of their gratitude. Everything you see conveys connection, warmth, kindness, forgiveness, caregiving, comfort. You breathe it in.

When you see the faces of those who are no longer in your life, the love you feel is tinged with the pain of loss. But the memory of loving connection remains, and you realize that all your love relationships serve as coordinates for your journey. They lend identity, grounding, and balance. Even more, they are vehicles for a deeper, more transcendent love that lies behind them all. In comparison to this Divine essence, however, they are transient, provisional, and pale.

As each face appears within the flames, you feel compelled to speak a new kind of freedom into these relationships, simply by letting go of your own neediness. "I don't need your approval to be happy," you say softly. "I don't need to cling to you to feel secure. I don't need to shape your behavior. I love you as you are." As you remove your own neediness from the equation, you see more clearly what the other individuals in your life might need. What might they need to hear from you? Where might they need some space? What might they need you to let go of in the relationship? As you ponder these questions, new insights and subtle intuitions come to you from your newfound nonattached perspective. This is the space from which grace flows out.

Finally, you exhale and return to the present. The external world comes into focus once more, and your senses come alive. The chirp of the cricket comes back into your awareness, along with the movement of some animal in a distant thicket, the soft rustle of the leaves.

With another deep sigh of release, you turn back to the book in your lap, continuing to read the teachings of the mystics, their stories of suffering and transcendence. Whenever something strikes you, you pause to reflect, to allow new ideas room to grow within you before you read on.

Then a snap of a twig and the crunch of small stones startles you. You look up to see that the man from earlier in the evening, the man who handed you the book, is approaching. He's alone now, his cowl drawn back behind his head. You feel both drawn to his presence and at the same time a sense of foreboding. Does he want the book back?

As he draws near to you, you stand and extend the book to him. He waves his hand and motions for you to sit again, and then he too takes a seat beside the fire. Firelight flickers on his robe, casts his shadow out long behind him. When you meet his eyes, his gaze is steady, warm, earnest. For a short time, he simply looks at you with soft eyes, a deep knowing there, firelight playing off his craggy face. You feel a sense of expectancy, as though you are suspended between thoughts, uncertain how to proceed.

After a time, he straightens his back, closes his eyes, and takes a deep breath. You take this as a cue to follow suit. You too inhale, close your eyes, and return to an inner space.

WAYPOST 9 EXERCISES

Select **at least two** exercises:

1. **The Release:** List the three relationships you depend on most for your psychological well-being. Then list the three things in life that provide you with the greatest sense of stability. Finally, list the three people with whom you've felt most in conflict or competition in your life. For the first group, visualize each person and tell him or her, *"I do not need your approval to be fulfilled."* For the second group, visualize each thing, habit, group, activity, identity or institution, and say, *"I do not need this in my life to be fulfilled."* For the third group, visualize each person and say, *"I do not need to be better than you to be fulfilled."* Which of these statements affected you the most? What insight did you gain from this exercise?

2. **Visio Divina:** Take a close look at *Trinity Icon* by Andrei Rublev and *The Return of the Prodigal Son* by Rembrandt. Read the background to these paintings. How do these paintings depict aspects of love?

3. **Poetica Divina:** Read the poems "Effortlessly" by Mechtild of Magdeburg, "The Avowal" by Denise

Levertov, "Wild Geese" by Mary Oliver, and "One Whisper of the Beloved" by Rumi. What do these poems reveal about agape-love? What resonated with you most?

4. **Audio Divina:** Listen to a song that invokes unconditional love for you. (My selections: "Pride (In the Name of Love) "by U2, "You've Been Loved" by Joseph Arthur, "I Grieve" by Peter Gabriel.)

5. **Lectio Divina:** Matthew 5:43–48 (Read, Reflect, Respond, *Rest*).

NOTES

1. Anthony De Mello. *Awareness: Conversations with the Masters* (New York: Crown Publishing, 2011), page 173.

2. Ken Wilber. *Grace and Grit: Spirituality and Healing in the Life and Death of Treya Killam Wilber* (Boulder, CO: Shambhala, 2001), page 68.

3. Llewellyn Vaughan-Lee. *The Paradoxes of Love* (Inverness, CA: The Golden Sufi Center Publishing, 1996), page 15.

4. "For now we see through a glass, darkly; but then face to face: now I know in part; but then shall I know even as also I am known" (1 Corinthians 13:12 KJV).

5. This term was first used by the sixteenth-century mystic Saint John of the Cross, referring to the periods of spiritual and emotional darkness he believed were necessary to the

soul on the path to Divine union. John of the Cross wrote that these times of spiritual purging are typical of the first of the three stages in what he described as the mystical journey, followed by the stages of illumination and then union. Notice how these compare to the structure of Dante's road.

6. Matthew 5:45.

7. Dionysius wrote, "Now it seems to me that those who have been purified . . . should give up their superabundant purity to others . . . should spread their overflowing light everywhere" (*Pseudo-Dionysius: The Complete Works* [Mahwah, NJ: Paulist Press, 1987], page 155). This mysterious fifth-century author (Dionysius was his pseudonym and his real identity is unknown) may have been one of the earliest mystics to describe the spiritual journey in terms of the three stages of purification, illumination, and what he refers to as perfection.

8. Anthony De Mello. "Wake Up Spirituality for Today," https://demellospirituality.com/2018/03/11/wake-up-spirituality-for-today.

9. As Paul wrote in his letter to the Ephesians, "Neither death, nor life, nor angels, nor principalities, nor powers, nor things present, nor things to come, Nor height, nor depth, nor any other creature, shall be able to separate us from the love of God" (8:38–39 KJV).

10. Philippians 4:7 KJV.

11. *Tehom* is the Hebrew word used in the Bible to refer to "the deep" or the "abyss," the place from which issued the primordial waters of creation.

At the center of our being is a point of nothing-ness which is untouched by sin and by illusion, a point of pure truth, a point or spark which belongs entirely to God.

-THOMAS MERTON

The mystical path is a journey from separation to union from multiplicity to Oneness.

-LLEWELLYN VAUGHAN-LEE

Contemplative prayer is the opening of mind and heart, our whole being, to God, the Ultimate Mystery, beyond thoughts, words, and emotions. It is a process of interior purification that leads, if we consent, to divine union.

-FATHER THOMAS KEATING

Into the Divine Union

Waypost 10

At the end of Dante's journey, he has an overwhelming vision of brilliant light and Divine grace. He comes to a realm beyond the physical and is suddenly swathed in a living light that gives him new powers of perception. He now sees the luminescent bodies around him. But everything is hazy. His guide explains that a profound purity is required to see this highest heavenly image of majestic grace and love—the rose of flame.

The contemplative mystic St. Bernard of Clairvaux appears before Dante in this new realm. He will now serve as Dante's guide, while Beatrice resumes her place on the petals of the rose that is emerging into view. Sent by prayer and light, Bernard prepares Dante for his final vision of heavenly radiance at the heart of the rose. He lovingly guides Dante through the rose and explains how each spirit is provided a place there. Dante discovers that each Divine figure he met along his journey through the Paradiso mysteriously also inhabits a petal on this rose.

In this space of Divine grace, Dante now wants to look as far as his gaze can penetrate into the highest light at the very center of the rose, that of Christ himself. Doing so requires prayer for grace and intercession. Bernard prays that Mary will help Dante receive this grand vision of the transcendent principle that holds together the very fabric of reality.

Granted the Divine revelation for which he longs, Dante is enraptured, gazing steadfast and motionless into this ever-growing radiance. The nature and shape of reality open themselves to him, the great mysteries of the relationship of the Divine to the human form. Dante sees that Divine reality is both constant and changing, self-knowing and self-revealing, with the seemingly scattered forms of creation bound by love into a single whole. This is a wholesale immersion into the Divine Being.

The effect of seeing such a vision, to have this taste of God, is to be unable to cast it aside for anything else.

It satisfies every longing, every hunger, every desire. Dante realizes he himself is part of this Divine dance. Caught up in the vision of perfect circles of Divine Love, he sees that he too is *moved by that same Love that moves the sun and other stars*. His inmost being is integrated into Divine life.

In being granted this insight into Ultimate Reality, Dante perceives the transcendent beauty of a creation both unified by love and also cast into a multiplicity of forms. Humbled as well as transfigured, he recognizes the inadequacy of thought and language to capture the essence of this Divine reality that is always at play. He is in a space of wholeness, grace, love, and perfection. Of union.

He's come *home*.

IMAGINE

You sit beneath the stars, in silent presence. Across the fire sits the monk with eyes shut, breathing slowly and evenly. Time draws out.

Thoughts come to you of the journey you've been on, the visions you've seen of personal shame and personal grace. All the while you have a dim awareness of emotions and sensations at the edge of your perception. For a moment, you become distracted and open your eyes. The monk's eyes open also, and his gaze meets yours.

In the firelight, his eyes seem radiant, ablaze, as if they are looking through you. His gaze is both fearsome and loving, destructive and life giving. You feel seen, known, exposed, as if this mysterious man knows your entire story—every misstep, every failure, every fear. But instead of causing anxiety, you see these flaws as he might, this silent stranger in whom you sense a deep wisdom. You have a sense not only of being seen completely, but another sensation of being loved unconditionally. You are both laid bare and entirely held.

You continue in this way, aligning your vision with his. With him, you see everything that's happened to you. Every choice you've made. Every attachment. Every relationship. Every addiction. Every recovery. Every achievement. Every failure. Every loss. Every gain. All is held in the warmth of your shared gaze.

Time seems suspended, as though there is only this moment. You sense a connection to the things around you: the breath of a breeze that moves through the grass, the stars overhead, a sliver of a moon, the crackle of the fire. Then, this outer perception falls away. Your awareness moves from your inner space of emotion and memory to your body, then outward to the immediate surroundings, then wider, to the path you took, to the mountain itself, to the bustle of the city, to the light-filled forest, to the quiet abbey, to the cave, to the dark passages you've taken. All reality is bathed in a blazing love. It seems to permeate all living things. It is even mysteriously present in the spaces in between.

In this chapter, we want to honor the sense of arrival, of homecoming, that comes from abiding in silence. This deep recognition of the nature of both the world and ourselves creates an ever-deepening connection between our inmost self and the Divine nature. It allows us to remain rooted in the awareness of an ever-present Divine love, and to manifest this quality in the world.

This is what the mystics call Divine union. In the inner silence we come home to our very selves—the place where the union, the consummation takes place. In doing so, the seat of the self experiences a wholesale shift. We partake of a greater pattern of inner annihilation, the inner death that leads to a fullness of life in which our very understanding of ourselves, the world, God, and the relationship between these is transformed.

As we ascend the spiritual path, we can expect a corresponding descent back down into the depths of our being and into the darkness of experience. Even though we are never the same after this awakening, this essential insight, we will still be required to face further challenges, to take further journeys into the inner depths. We paradoxically recognize both our own inherent wholeness and the continuous need to let go in order to abide in that state of awareness. Having traveled this road before, now we can trust that the overall movement is that of a greater excavation, a hollowing out that makes space for the Divine indwelling.

The spiritual movement isn't a linear one, but a process of ongoing deepening and expanding, of contraction and release. New revelations await. As we align with the Divine perspective more and more, we understand that in spite of whatever pain or difficulty that may arise, it is all part of the journey. We don't turn the pain into an identity. Instead, we identify with the silent observer, the witness, and practice the Divine perspective of unitive seeing, perceiving our individual selves as part of a greater whole at all times. We are content for this greater whole to unfold from the Divine perspective, conjoined in love, aware at all times that yet another Dark Night of the Soul may guide us into more perfect union.

On my own journey, I had made what felt like great strides. I practiced daily Centering Prayer and Lectio Divina when possible; I had entered into a twelve-step program that provided community and accountability;

and I rediscovered a deep and genuine inner joy and purpose and presence.

Then changes came. My schedule became oriented around work and a newborn. My wife and I were trading off nighttime feedings, so at least one of us would be guaranteed a night's sleep, but my normal rhythms were all suspended. After a number of months, deprived of sleep, daily contemplative practice, and a regular schedule, some of the inner infrastructure I'd built up began to crack.

During this time, I went through periods of great acceptance and freedom that were followed by times of rising resistance, anger, and resentment. The old mental tapes would begin to play their message: *I'm not getting what I need and I never will.* The sense returned of a separate self that deserved to have its own emotional needs met. The days became a slog again. The old addictions started to come back. The deep feelings of loneliness and rejection returned. The sense of entitlement to a hidden inner life crept back as well, draining vitality and energy from me as it had before. Inner dissonance settled over me again, the longing for *something else,* for escape. It was debilitating to fall into patterns I thought I had overcome or moved beyond.

Sooner or later, life's normal frustrations will always trigger the core wound once again. In my case, fortunately, a friend recommended the writings of several mystics, both ancient and modern. After reading and reflecting, praying and sitting with my old familiar processes, I experienced a profound inner release and acceptance. I had been experiencing life as a constructed self that was situated inside a melodrama, but now it was as if an overinflated balloon finally burst. All inner tension was gone. I had a fresh awakening experience as I recognized the extent to which I was entrapped in concepts, social conventions, conditioning, and attachments.

With this inner shift, there was suddenly no shame. No fear. No anger. No resentment. In their place was a simple joy. A recognition that without projected desire, happiness didn't depend on anything external, nor would any external circumstance provide any kind of lasting fulfillment. What I had known at a conceptual or hoped-for level was now a genuine inner experience. With a new sense of lightness, I rested in complete and utter peace. Aware that I was held in an abiding love, I recognized the source of my own wholeness.

I understood that all the things I had craved—getting my attachments right, having my needs met, getting even, a new relationship, the right achievement or community, any form of affection or esteem—could be viewed in the context of great freedom as I saw these desires as if from a Divine perspective. Nothing external in the temporal sphere could provide this deep and lasting peace.

As I patiently watched my mental-emotional patterns from a detached but gracious and loving perspective, I experienced an inrush of energy that lasted for several days. During this time, I received insights into my own path, my own struggle, and a framework to understand the paths of others. I felt greater compassion for their struggles as well. Like sudden flashbulbs, the memory of various passages of scripture would burst into my consciousness, accompanied by a greater sense of their inner meaning. These passages had to do with letting go of the illusion of identity, of possessions, of status, of family, of worrying about past and future . . . of surrendering to the Divine reality.

This new and brighter light was a kind of retroactive grace shining into the memories of my darkest days. It set into perspective my struggle with my shadow side and with addiction. These now became processes of refinement to release the ego's hold. All my frustration and resentment, pain and depression became the means to arrive at a sense of selflessness. In this state of desirelessness, Divine life flowed, a prevenient joy, a sense of loving interconnectedness with all creation.

I had experiential insight into the way in which our lives are mysteriously both a journey and an eternal essence. We grow and mature on the one hand, and we partake of an unchanging Divine nature on the other. Our inmost essence is a perpetual and steady spirit, and yet we participate in this outer world of form. Neither cancels out the other.

Our experience, our *home*, is this ever-present moment. When we slip into a consciousness that deviates from that moment and look to find fulfillment in the past, in the future, or in contrived dramas, we fall back into egoic patterns and self-imposed suffering. We wander away from *home*. With this new understanding, I began to pay closer attention to any sense of inner discontent or resistance. Usually, I could trace it to an involuntary, reactive thought process. Identifying it and letting it go meant a return to natural joy, to the original blessing of the present moment.

We give up our natural state, our birthright of exquisite joy and freedom, for thought-forms and concepts, desires and attachments, for stories we've made up. Instead of taking Dante's road to union with the Divine, we follow the ways in which we are conditioned to seek fulfillment. Some of us are so identified with our thought patterns, with the voices in our heads, that we never have a moment's true peace. We never penetrate the veil of surfaces, never pull out to the wide shot of our inner world where we see all our need, worry, and egoic games like a self-contained planet floating in space. We never experience the freedom of disidentifying from this small self.

During this time in my own life, my life laid bare and excavated, I received an infusion of Divine grace, a sense of gentleness, patience, peace, joy, and most of all *love*. I was able to see life as a channel, a vessel for bringing this kind of love into the world, complete and unconditional. This love transcends our tribal affiliations, transcends our limited conditioning, transcends our limiting concepts and language.

My experience gradually went from an intense inner vibrancy and vitality, enthusiasm, energy, and flashes of intuitive insight, to a kind of neutral zone of abiding peace and inner acceptance of reality moment to moment, with a high degree of awareness of both inner and outer realities. I could see triggers or treacherous thoughts as they arose, as the ego felt threatened or tried to latch on to some slight or dismissal. It was as if I could sense emotions and thoughts in my perceptual field like a physical object, a deviation from the inner equilibrium I'd found, a ripple on the inner lake of peace—and once I noticed them, I could let them go. I could see unconscious dynamics at work in others, too, and instead of trying to change them myself, I could allow a peaceful, gracious awareness flow through me into our interactions—and then accept the results, whatever they were.

To make sense of my experience, I read more deeply from the mystics who explore this territory in depth. Different mystics use different language, but they all describe the experience of inner release. Christian mystics refer to it as the Kingdom of God and interpret several of Christ's teachings in this light. Others describe this state of being as the Inner Witness, Presence, or present-moment-awareness; Presence is only interested in what love asks of us right now. I dove into the writings of Pseudo-Dionysius, who describes the threefold contemplative path of purgation, illumination, and union. I found that centuries later, the twentieth-century mystic Evelyn Underhill picked up the same threads, which then drew me back to mystics throughout the centuries.

In each case, the journey to wholeness was triggered by prolonged inner suffering or tension. This corresponded to my own inner experience, a movement from wound to wholeness, a state of grace that was not something I had acquired but rather what was left when all other striving had been let go. Mystics like John of the Cross described this state as Divine union:

What God communicates to the soul in this intimate union is totally beyond words. One can say nothing about it just as one can say nothing about God Himself that resembles Him. For in the transformation of the soul in God, it is God who communicates Himself with admirable glory. In this transformation, the two become one, as we would say of the window united with the ray of sunlight, or of the coal with the fire, or of the starlight with the light of the Sun.[1]

The consistent message of the connection from silence to transformation to Divine union is woven through the writings of the mystics and contemplatives. Fifth-century mystic Dionysius the Areopagite writes:

The higher we soar in contemplation, the more limited become our expressions of that which is purely intelligible; even as now, when plunging into the Darkness which is above the intellect, we pass not merely into brevity of speech, but even into absolute silence, of thoughts as well as of words . . . and, according to the degree of transcendence, so our speech is restrained until, the entire ascent being accomplished, we become wholly voiceless, inasmuch as we are absorbed in Him who is totally ineffable.[2]

Trappist monk Thomas Keating goes so far as to remind us that "silence is God's first language; everything else is a poor translation."[3] This is in part because as soon as we use language, we invoke an implied cultural context, with its tribal identities and normative value systems. Caught within the linguistic layer only, we define and distinguish, differentiate self and other, construct a mental story about ourselves within that context. Genuine spirit transcends all those provisional structures. Awakening means recognizing the primacy of that which is beyond language and concept. Language can only provide a map; it frames reality. But language always falls short of Divine mystery.

And so, in silence we open ourselves to a much deeper transformation than is possible or accessible through language. There is a sweetness we detect in the silence. This is not only the absence of noise, but also the absence of striving, of thought, of clamor. Virtues, graces, and fruits of the spirit—these are born and cultivated in silence.

As entering into this inner silence becomes a habit, we become far more aware of the deviations we habitually make from that tranquility. Yes, things still happen in our day-to-day lives: we lose the keys or we are late for an appointment; we experience a sense of lack, or fear, or even depression. But this transpires within the context of a vast inner silence. Emotions become like the drama of heavenly bodies: yes, stars explode, asteroids collide, nebula expand, new stars form, but all this plays out against the boundless backdrop of an infinite space. An infinite silence. A Divine silence. In this silence we simply rest in the presence of God. In silence, our inmost self comes *home*.

As we sit in daily contemplative practice, we intentionally withdraw our focus from the perpetual-motion faculty of the mind and enter into the silence. For many, this seemingly simple act can be daunting. We're used to distracting ourselves, staying busy, using the noise of daily life to avoid the inner dissatisfaction. Within this space of silence, however, even as thoughts and emotions arise and the mind wanders, we can become aware of these distractions and then simply let them go.

In Centering Prayer, we repeat a sacred word to help signal to our brains a return to silence and a consent to the presence and action of God within. As this becomes more and more of a habit, we grow more aware of the transient nature of the thoughts and emotions with which we habitually identify. Then, once we've allowed a bit of space to emerge between our observing presence and the thought-forms, we begin realigning our identity from this small self, the bundle of perception, thought, and emotion, to the spacious backdrop against which they play out.

This state of being has no ideological statement. It is not a belief system. It's simply what happens when we let go of all the provisional bits and pieces that make up our sense of self. A name, a nationality, a marriage, a residence, a history. With practice, we literally move into a different state of consciousness where these words become irrelevant. As we put space between our ourselves and the concepts of self that bedevil us (according to which we swing between success and failure, meaning and meaninglessness), we find a deep and genuine rest. For a moment, we take joy in just being.

In the early stages, this level of awareness ebbs and flows. In my own life, for example, the current realities of my life can interfere with my daily practice of Centering Prayer. Full-time work, raising an active child, and being married to a high-energy wife with a demanding job all challenge my inner balance on a daily basis. As things are now, I don't have a gap in my schedule to take a week here or there for deep spiritual immersion on a contemplative retreat. Old thought patterns, challenges, and reactive patterns are still there. But rather than identifying with these, rather than saying I *am* depressed and falling into deeper despair, I'm aware that, ultimately, this is not me. Depression is here.

Depression is happening. But it isn't essentially *me*. My deepest self is far vaster than this transient experience of depression that's moving through like a storm. It's only the temporary weather of my life, not the overall climate.

And these feelings then become cues to ask myself: Where is this coming from? What root needs to be pulled out? What attachment or unmet expectation is causing this? What change does love require in this situation? Ego continues to creep into my life, but I make a practice of shifting my center of gravity back to loving acceptance.

I also have periods of profound grace, during which I'm seemingly borne along, able to appreciate the sweetness of the moment, accepting reality as it is without resisting, pursuing, or judging. During these times, my mind's normal patterns—finding problems to fixate on, to complain about, to resent, or to anticipate and prepare for—disappears. Instead, I'm simply present and open to an abundant delight in what is. I recognize that I am already complete, already whole.

When we recognize our essential wholeness, we see problems in a new light. This shift is like diving down into the ocean in a storm. The waves of the mind are still there, but from this vast interior space, they are no longer threatening. I can still take decisive action in the world or recognize that something has to change; acceptance isn't resignation. But my choices come out of inner clarity rather than inner turmoil.

This is the fruit of an ongoing contemplative practice. And although the particular experience of Divine union is unique to each individual, it does seem to be characterized by several consistent threads or patterns in the lives, writings, and teachings of the mystics and contemplatives.

One of these threads is an embrace of paradox and mystery, while the need to define truth in static concepts and language drops away. Immersion in the contemplative path opens us up to the mysterious contradictions that underlie our experience.

One paradox we experience is that we live both in eternity and in a specific context. We return from moments of transcendence to a body, a set of perceptions, thoughts, experiences, and memory. We go back to our life situation. But as contemplatives, we do not despise the body or the environment as obstacles to connecting with spirit. Instead, we recognize they are part of our curriculum. They are the vehicles of awakening to the Divine reality. And just as the body goes through phases of waking and sleeping, growth, decay, and death, so too does our awareness of spiritual reality.

In moments of contemplation, we experience life in full, untethered by past and future, by our ideas of who we are or ought to be. We connect to a reality both deeper and transcendent. We are both spirit and matter, formlessness and form, self and no-self. The one doesn't cancel out the other. All our experience becomes grist for the mill, each challenge an opportunity to dissolve ego and become aligned with loving presence.

For most of us, this doesn't mean we get shiny white robes and start to levitate in the lotus position. We're still in the thick of things. We spill the milk. We lose our phone. We get stuck in traffic. We experience a moment of anger or frustration, or a bout of depression. But in each case, our contemplative practice allows us to maintain a sense of disidentification from these experiences; we understand that it will pass. We no longer live in a reactive state, and—gradually or suddenly— we begin to laugh at the things that used to make us angry.

Jesus teaches this kind of radical responsibility for our inner state when he tells us to clean the inside of the cup so the outside may become clean as well,[4] or to turn the other cheek and give our shirt to someone who steals our cloak.[5] When we're not identified with our ego, what is there to be angry at when someone insults it? What do we have to lose?

Another characteristic of so many of the mystics and contemplatives is they seem to carry a different sense of time. It's as if they're more attuned to the slow movement of geological time than the current news cycle. While we often get caught up in the latest scandal or enmeshed in political in-fighting, the mystics are able to maintain calm and balance, recognizing the immediate issues as only momentary troubles.

Some contemplatives suggest exercises such as imagining our own death and our decaying body as the means to entering this awareness of deep time. As we die, the stars will still wheel about. The sun will still rise. Other mystics suggest picturing the place we're sitting now as it was one hundred years ago, envisioning it as vividly as we can, then a thousand years ago, then ten thousand years ago. What did it look like? What sounds would have been heard? What might it have felt like? This exercise expands our awareness beyond our immediate emotional reality, which is no reality at all. Against the vastness of geological time, not to mention the chronology of the universe, our normal concerns and preoccupations take a much different scope. As Richard Rohr puts it, "to be a contemplative is to learn how to trust deep time and to learn how to rest there, and not be wrapped up in chronological time, because what you learn is that all of it passes away."[6]

Living in light of this awareness allows us to go about our daily lives with a good deal more patience and graciousness for the little obstacles we encounter. Entering deep time releases us from our usual egocentric consciousness. We realize there is a vast and wondrous creation sustained by forces far beyond our ability to control or influence. Although the ego panics in the face of this kind of annihilation, feeling trivialized and redundant, the spirit rests in this awareness. Ultimately, there's nothing to prove nor achieve. In spirit, in deep time, we are already complete, already whole, already home. We're paradoxically freed from our emotional entanglement to fully inhabit the moment we're in.

Another characteristic of the mystic's consciousness is nonduality. In our default state, we tend to perceive the world dualistically, creating simplistic categories to navigate the world and to consolidate our own ego identity. But contemplative practice diminishes our need to label, to judge, to reject, to define ourselves through differentiation. Most of us organize information we receive into mental categories with our own egoic identity as the organizing principle. Call it our mental infrastructure. Dualistic ways of thinking create abstract categories and then compare and contrast those categories. We evaluate, accept, and reject based on these categories. Then we also have an active ego structure that has a relationship to these various categories, that defines itself by some and in rejection of others. The nondual witness we cultivate in contemplation observes this process at work as if from the macro level. It's like seeing a maze from a bird's-eye view. Nonduality is a corrective for our normal way of processing, learning, and perceiving.

Many of the categories we use are, of course, perfectly natural, useful, and necessary for navigating life. Nondual mind doesn't reject dualistic thinking as bad, just as limited. It's appropriate for the practical sphere of life but leaves us impotent in the face of mysteries like the sacred and the holy, like death and eternity and wholeness. With practice, our normal mental categories are suspended, shot through and flooded with love. We understand they are provisional, conditioned, temporary. In light of the mystical experience, we reevaluate our categories and ask: does this thought, belief, or category serve the needs of love?

The contemplative dimension adds an entirely new level of perception. By intentionally removing our automatic evaluative faculty—the mind—and consenting to God's presence as a regular habit, we are empowered to adopt a Divine perspective. Our being, and therefore the level of consciousness through which we habitually perceive, becomes transformed. We gain the ability to set aside the ego that is constantly looking for an edge or an identity, supremacy or fulfillment, and instead *just see*. We become subject to new insights, new experiences, and fresh perceptions.

Nondual awareness or unitive seeing transcends our usual patterns of perception and description, which normally occur from the position of our small self. From this macro-level perspective, we can open to the reality and subtlety of any given situation, without reading our own categories into it.

As I think about this concept, what comes to mind is the way in which I interacted with stories when I was growing up. As a kid, I read mostly comic books, which usually had clear heroes and villains. When I started reading short stories and novels in school, at first I was constantly looking for clues as to who was the hero and who the villain. That was the prefabricated narrative into which I was attempting to fit the characters. Before I could invest in the characters and the story, I was waiting for the hero to show up. More mature fiction, of course, has nuanced and complex characters that require a greater sensitivity, understanding, and language to access and understand than more simplistic, naïve, or sentimental stories. This is often the difference between children's fiction and adult writing.

The first may rely on stock characters presented with a simple moral lesson, while adult literature conveys larger and more complex realities.

Many of us are still using an immature lens to interpret the world. We have our prefabricated story structures into which we want to fit reality—but the reality in which we live is actually far more multifaceted. Part of an abundant life is being sensitive to those nuances, seeing reality as it is, without imposing ready-made categories onto the characters around us.

Nondual awareness also means *seeing with the eyes of the heart*. It has a quality of openheartedness that comes from an alignment and attunement between head and heart. We experience life and immediate situations with the whole in mind. We understand that we are all partakers in the Divine nature—and waking up to this reality is what the journey is about. This is the highest level of spiritual attainment as mapped out by the Christian contemplative tradition's threefold path of purgation, illumination, and union.

Another aspect of the contemplative life is recognizing that everyone is at a different stage of development and maturity. Just as each of us has passed through different stages on our spiritual journey, we bring empathy, understanding, and compassion to others on their own journey. Like Dante, mystics and contemplatives with deep spiritual insight have framed the spiritual life in terms of progressive stages. From Dionysius's three-fold path to St. Bernard's *Four Loves* to the writings of Teresa of Avila and John of the Cross, the depiction is consistently that of *ascent* or a climb up to a higher state of awareness. Modern spiritual writers continue this tradition. Trappist monk Thomas Merton's autobiography is titled *The Seven Storey Mountain*, invoking the imagery of Dante's Purgatory. Thomas Keating echoes St. Teresa and St. John of the Cross in much of his writing, likening the soul's journey toward God to the *Ascent of Mt. Carmel*. Applying principles of modern scholarship, James Fowler identifies seven stages of faith.[7] Just as we develop socially and emotionally, it seems we also develop our spiritual faculties in progressive stages. The purpose of this development is to reach what is called Divine union, unitive consciousness, or Oneness. We are all climbing toward the same goal—but we may progress at different speeds. Perhaps that is partly because in union with the Divine we retain our distinctive personhood, our gifts and temperaments. Fourth-century mystic Gregory of Nyssa expressed it this way:

> The distinction between the persons does not impair the oneness of nature, nor does the shared unity of essence lead to a confusion between the distinctive

characteristics of the persons. Do not be surprised that we should speak of the Godhead as being at the same time both unified and differentiated. Using riddles, as it were, we envisage a strange and paradoxical diversity-in-unity and unity-in-diversity.[8]

The contemplative transformation is at once profoundly private and universal. It allows us to recognize our inherent interconnectedness, our oneness, and knits us together with the whole, even while we maintain our distinctiveness.

Some of us may have mystical experiences in which the veil between our sense of self, creation, and God seems to disappear. We feel at one with all, partaking of the flow of the Divine nature. This can be a profound and overpowering experience accompanied by an inflow of energy and creativity. It moves us along in our journey and reveals the genuine power of Divine reality. Although the boundaried self has not permanently dissolved and become conjoined to the Divine will, nevertheless, we are partakers of the Divine nature in our inmost essence; we are in fact, along with Christ, the light of the world.

Yet another key characteristic of mystics and contemplatives is that once they have journeyed from wound-centered living to Divine union, they are drawn toward action and service. From the outside perspective, contemplative practice is often misconstrued as quietism, escapism, or navel gazing. In reality, however, this practice brings about the inner transformation that empowers and energizes us, so that we become active channels of grace. After Francis of Assisi experienced an inner transformation, he committed to a life of poverty and served the poor—and spiritual aspirants, laypeople, and according to legend, even the animals were drawn to him. St. Ignatius had a similar experience of transformation, catalyzed by a physical wound, followed by a harrowing experience in a cave where he confronted his shadow self, and finally achieved a Divine union that allowed him to become a living conduit for grace. He founded the Society of Jesus, or the Jesuits, whom he envisioned as "contemplatives in action." In the 1500s, he developed the Spiritual Exercises still used in spiritual direction and retreats to this day.

On my own path, having undergone a process of transformation has vastly expanded my horizons. Usually preoccupied and insular or concerned with the small tribe with which I identify, I've become connected to other people and other spiritual traditions. In pursuing contemplative community, I've learned from Sufi mystics, Franciscan Celtic monastics, Integral

Spirituality teachers, twelve-step attendees, and Protestant spiritual directors. I've learned that Zen monks like Wolfgang Kopp also know something of the Divine union the Christian mystics describe. Kopp writes:

> Without this spiritual longing, we will never be capable of the all-consuming love that culminates in absolute surrender to the divine. This absolute surrender is a total self-dissolution or kenosis, as in the example of Jesus Christ, who lived his self-dissolving love to the point of crucifixion. To become like Him in self-dissolution is the unqualified prerequisite to *unio mystica,* the union with God.[9]

Despite the common threads that connect all mystics, the contemplative path doesn't emphasize a set of texts or principles we have to accept to be part of the group. It's not a conversion project to a way of thinking or belief, using a specific set of language, concepts, and categories. Instead, we undergo the process of dying to our False Self and then we simply look, see, observe. We stay attuned to the Divine presence in the moment. We are interested in introducing this presence, perspective, and work of love into each situation as much as we can. We've irreversibly shifted the seat of selfhood and identity, our source of meaning and fulfillment.

We embrace and live with paradox. The dualisms dissolve and we recognize that all states exist on a continuum. We seek to dwell in an abiding peace and to bring that to each interaction, allowing natural qualities of joy, acceptance, forgiveness, and transformation to flow out of that space. In terms of specific religious beliefs, we gradually became far less interested in arguing for one theological position over another, for one tradition over another. We begin to understand that such arguments are actually only defenses against perceived ego threats.

No matter what transformation we experience, we seem to arrive where others before us have walked and can draw comfort, strength, and wisdom from a sense of renewed and expanded community. Out of these relationships, new opportunities to serve arise. Through connecting with interfaith spiritual directors, I've facilitated weekend retreats with men transitioning out of homelessness at a Jesuit retreat center. Through my local Presbyterian church, I've been involved in spiritual direction workshops and retreats. I work with groups to bring contemplative practices into local prisons with a Trappist contemplative organization.

In each case, as we follow Dante's road—this same path the mystics and contemplatives have also walked—we enter the darkness to see the light. The walls we build with our minds begin to dissolve. Fed by those moments of deep awareness of connection to the Divine nature, abiding Divine presence, and inherent wholeness, we're oriented toward those in need of movement, of transformational insight. We receive wisdom and guidance from others who walk before us, regardless of their tribal affiliations. In doing so, we seldom see any fireworks. Freed from our demanding ego, we realize, however, that we don't need fireworks.

Contemplative practice recognizes that our responses in real-life situations register in the body. If we have a thought with an emotional charge—an embarrassing moment, an argument, a break up, a loss—we respond both emotionally and physically. We experience tension somewhere in the body. And unlike a belief or ideology, which exists only in the mind, contemplative practices like Centering Prayer counter our emotional and physical responses with a physiological gesture of letting go. Through paying attention to the thought and the physical sensations, we enter into a neutral space of observation where we can surrender the whole game of reactivity. This game is a common obstacle to participation in the Divine life. However, as we surrender thought by thought, emotion by emotion, moment by moment, we allow ourselves to be stitched back together, reintegrated, made whole.

No belief or ideology can do this for us. Without the practice itself, we find ourselves once more taking our regular low-level reactive consciousness into the world, intent on threat detection. We try to live in wisdom, to put on the mind of Christ, and to love our enemy—but we are still using the old operating system. Without contemplative practices to grow into this quality of being, we assume our failures are aspects of the normal spiritual experience—so we just keep asking forgiveness for our shortcomings, rather than actually becoming loving agents of wholeness. Drawn up into the Divine life, however, we become reflections of the Divine radiance without getting enmeshed in the ego dynamics of ourselves or others. We aren't nostalgic about the past, anxious about the future, or desiring anything from anyone. This is space beyond concept, beyond language. In this state, we are fully present and receptive. Free.

As we've already stated, arriving at this mode of being isn't a matter of attaining something outside ourselves or achieving the favor of God to bestow this blessing on us. Instead, as teacher James Finley says, "I cannot make moments of nondual consciousness happen. I can only assume the inner stance that offers the least resistance to being overtaken by grace."[10] The contemplative experience that leads toward awareness, wholeness, and Divine union is precisely this pure grace. It is an inflow of the ever-present, superordinate Divine reality.

Throughout the ages, mystics have held that there are certain practices or methods that can help us open ourselves to this experience. Strictly speaking, though, the method itself is never the experience of contemplation. The method is merely a process of openness, of signaling consent. The experience of contemplative prayer is pure gift. Our spiritual hunger is like God knocking at the door. A method like Centering Prayer is us responding by opening the door. What enters then is Divine grace.

From the contemplative perspective, this grace is ever-present; all that's required is our consent to it. We often keep it at bay when we fall back into the default level of egoic consciousness, when society's voice and values lead us around by the nose, or when we pay more attention to the misleading tapes in our head. That's why the practice of consciously entering into silence is so important. This physical, embodied gesture of relinquishing literally changes our neural pathways, which are habitually responding to stimuli around us.[11] Normally, a threat alert in our emotional centers pushes us into reactive mode, triggering a fight-or-flight response with a heightened propensity toward accusation, anger, self-justification. It takes practice and time to change those neural pathways and make room for the Divine indwelling in place of our animal reactivity. Cultivating a receptivity to the Divine requires inner work, commitment, diligence through long stretches of dryness, and attentive alertness.

The contemplative practice is like a love relationship—we move from acquaintanceship to friendship to intimate union. This doesn't make us immediately enlightened, but in bringing this newfound awareness into different social situations, we begin to see ourselves as we truly are in those contexts. We start to recognize the triggers and habit responses that contribute to our daily struggle. The benefits of contemplative practice are more evident throughout the rest of the day than during the time of practice itself.

On the contemplative path, we gradually begin to understand two separate definitions of the self: the *Me* who acts and the *I* who sees. These two selves correspond to the two levels of existence we described earlier in the chapter: the mental-physical world and the transcendent spiritual reality. The egoic *Me* exists on the level of mind, where the human drama unfolds with its drives, desires, and frustrations, its slings and arrows of outrageous fortune. The *I* participates in Divine awareness, out of which we are able to observe the Me as if from an objective, grace-filled vantage point. This certainly does not happen immediately, but the daily practice cultivates the capacity for this change to take place.

From the perspective of someone who has never experienced any of this, what I've described in this book can sound like nonsensical, wishful thinking, a set of overzealous propositions. From the perspective of spirit, though, it's anything but. Instead, it's the very heart of life's meaning—the Divine perspective and *experience* of Oneness.

The world opens up in a new way. Though on the surface we are still distinct and individual, beneath the surface, we are part of *all of it*, down to the smallest component. In moments of subtle awareness, we feel ourselves *identifying* with all of it. This capacity to diminish our separate self-sense, to loosen the ego's hold on us, to make room for Divine love and wisdom to flow through us, is the transforming union. This is the closest possible identification with God we can have in physical form.[12] It is paradoxically to become who we fully are. As Christ says, "If you try to hang on to your life, you will lose it. But if you give up your life for my sake, you will save it."[13]

Dante experiences this kind of ultimate alignment with Divine reality at the end of *The Divine Comedy* in his mystical vision:

now my will and my desire were turned,
like a wheel in perfect motion,
by the love that moves the sun and the other stars.

This is an image of the self in Divine union. The False Self has dissolved in the Divine light. Only the essence remains. We are truly home at last.

IMAGINE

As you sit by the fire, you feel the air warming, and through your eyelids, you see a hint of growing light. You open your eyes and see the stranger still across from you, looking at you again with an unbroken gaze. Dim light edges the horizon line; dawn is creeping into the world.

In the silence, the stranger slowly inhales, smiles, then closes his eyes again. You look around, take a breath, and close your eyes as well. Immediately, you have a sudden vision: You are standing in darkness on a low hillside overlooking a forest, the same forest where you once woke up. In the moonlight, you see yourself asleep. Then, as you watch, this other self turns and notices the stranger that sits beside you. After a moment of silence, the stranger begins singing, long and low and beautiful.

As you watch, the other two strangers who had been standing with him earlier step out of the shadows and join him. They too begin to sing, their voices weaving in harmony. After a moment, they motion for you to join them. You step alongside, face the forest valley, and sing. The song fills the valley and echoes off a rock face on the opposite side of the valley.

Then you recognize still another self there below, stirring beneath the foliage. This other self blinks and sits up, then tests the air with its nose. Still in your dream, you see others, scattered across the forest floor by the hundreds, all trapped in their own deep sleep. Here and there, a few begin to stir. The song moves through the trees. A breeze picks up, and some of the sleepers open their eyes and stretch. Some look about to find themselves, to get their bearings.

The song draws to a close and for a brief moment echoes in the valley. The men turn to you and gaze at you gently. Then the forest and the valley and the sleepers below begin to fade . . . and the vision is gone.

Filled with questions, you open your eyes. You turn to the stranger—but he's no longer there. When you look around for him you see only the fire, the hillside, the fading stars, the growing light. You relax back in your seat, filled now with both lightness and a sense of direction.

You know your path leads to the other side of the mountain into parts unknown, into undiscovered country. There will be sleepers there, you know. Or those who are just waking up. Or others farther along on their journey who have wisdom to teach you.

Sunlight spreads on the horizon. The valley stretches out below you, shrouded in morning mist, and beyond, peak glows on peak, as far as you can see. You get to your feet, breathe deep, and take your first step into the rest of this unfolding mystery.

WAYPOST 10 EXERCISES

Select **at least two** exercises:

1. **Immersion:** What activities do you engage in during which you are so immersed that you seem to lose a sense of a self? What is this experience like for you?

2. **Contemplative Practice:** During this week, practice one or more of the following practices *every day*, ideally first thing in the morning. After a bit of research, you will know what practice or practices best fit your current situation:
   a. **Centering Prayer** (See guidelines in Contemplative Practices section.)
   b. **The Jesus Prayer** (See guidelines in Contemplative Practices section.)

c. **Gratitude Pages** (First thing in the morning write down three things that happened the previous day that fill you with gratitude.)

3. **Create:** Create a poem, song, collage, painting, or your chosen medium around the topic of *silence*.

4. **Comparison:** Take a close look at the work of painter Robert Rauschenberg and composers John Cage and Arvo Pärt. Read the background to their work. How do these artists approach the territory of contemplation?

5. **Poetica Divina:** Read the poems "There Is a Field" by Rumi, "Empty Your Mind of All Thoughts" by Lao Tzu, and "Dark Night of the Soul" by John of the Cross (just the poem). What resonates with you most?

6. **Audio Divina:** Listen to songs that invokes a sense of the Divine or transcendent for you. (My selections: "Mystic" by Joshua James, "Für Hildegard von Bingen" by Devendra Banhart, and "Enlightenment" by Van Morrison.)

7. **Lectio Divina:** 1 Kings 19:11–13 (Read, Reflect, Respond, *Rest*).

NOTES

1. *The Collected Works of John of the Cross*, Kieran Kavanaugh and Otilio Rodriguez, trans. (Washington, DC: ICS, 1973), page 512.

2. Dionysus the Areopagite. *Theologia Mystica* (Godalming, UK: Shrine of Wisdom, 1923), chapter III. (Available online at http://www.esotericarchives.com/oracle/dionys1.htm.)

3. Thomas Keating. *Invitation to Love: The Way of Christian Contemplation* (A&C Black, 2012), page 105. Father Keating was quoting both the thirteenth-century Sufi mystic Rumi, who wrote, "Silence is the language of God. All else is poor translation," and John of the Cross, who wrote, "Silence is God's first language."

4. Matthew 23:26.

5. Mathew 5:38–40.

6. Richard Rohr made these comments in an interview with Krista Tippett for her *On Being* podcast on April 13, 2017. It's available online at https://onbeing.org/programs/richard-rohr-living-in-deep-time-apr2017/.

7. James Fowler. *Stages of Faith: The Psychology of Human Development and the Quest for Meaning* (San Francisco, CA: HarperOne, 1995).

8. From *Gregory of Nyssa's Mystical Writings*, translated and edited by Herbert Mursillo (Crestwood, NY: St. Vladimir's Seminary Press, 1979).

9. Wolfgang Kopp. *Free Yourself from Everything*, Barbara Wittenberg-Hasenauer, trans. (Rutland, VT: C.E. Tuttle Publishing, 1994).

10. This quote is from a blogpost titled "Overtaken by Oceanic

Oneness" by James Finley, posted on February 3, 2017, on the website of the Center for Action and Contemplation, https://cac.org/overtaken-oceanic-oneness-2017-02-03/.

11. Scientific studies using magnetic resonance imagery have found that regularly practicing some form of meditation does in fact change neural activity and brain structure. To read an overview of the many physiological benefits of meditation, see "Enlightened Neurons: Can Meditation Beef Up Brain Regions?" by Amy Kraft, World Science Festival, https://www.worldsciencefestival.com/2014/06/enlightened-neurons-can-meditation-beef-brain-regions/.

12. Though, as both scientists and the mystics suggest, the very nature of the body itself changes the more deeply we enter into this process.

13. Matthew 16:25 NLT.

Afterword

Rev. Karla Shaw,
Senior Pastor at Point Loma Community Presbyterian Church

"The Christian faith is not about getting answers to your questions, but about being held by a love so great that those questions neither create terror nor shame." This quote by an anonymous author was given to me by a pastor friend in Pittsburgh when I first entered the ministry, and it has hung on the fridge of my home ever since. It is a constant reminder to me of both the depth of God's love and the brutal honesty God calls us to in this journey we call life. Never be afraid to sit in the question.

When I first met Marc over lentil soup and red wine at an emerging Christian artist community in Los Angeles, shortly after I entered seminary in 2005, I had no idea that I would have the privilege of being his life partner through the ups and downs and ins and outs of the mysterious road of life and faith. Marc has always been a self-aware, at-ease philosopher of life, who can look past the surface of a person, situation, or text and see more, but his own journey with God and the shadows he has encountered, confronted, and released in himself have made him into what we call, in spiritual circles, a truly centered being.

I hope that this book has led you on a journey. This journey—Dante's road—is not an idea cooked up in a lab of ideals; it is the path of the Scriptures, the well-trod trail of the fathers and mothers who went before us. In our scattered and shallow world, few of us are willing to take this journey, though many of us want the end result.

If you are longing for freedom within, if the external changes that so many self-help authors and speakers tout as "life-changing" aren't working for you, if you want more for your life than a drudgery of false attachments and compartmentalization, then I encourage you to continue to ponder the ideas within this book. Turn back to it often in the months and years ahead. The process of change happens through internalizing these ideas—and then living them.

I have been an intimate witness to Marc's travels along the path he describes in this book. There is no other person I would trust more as a guide for this pilgrimage. I hope you experience what I have encountered through his wisdom and openness, as God meets you along the way.

Contemplative Practices

Recent contemplative writers have outlined three different layers of spiritual practice, bringing wholeness on the individual, communal, and greater social levels. The first kind of practice, like Centering Prayer, allows us to rest in the presence of God and experience inner transformation. The second, like Sabbath, confession, worship, and seasonal reflection, helps maintain the health of a community. The third, the service or missional practices, are meant to help move society itself toward wholeness or *shalom*. These would include work toward inclusion, peace, justice, and hospitality.

Since this book is intended for those beginning to undertake contemplative life and practice, we first have to clean out the inside of the cup (Matthew 23:26)—allow the inner transformation to take place. Our focus, then, is on contemplative practices for the individual, but the ultimate hope is that this transformation radiates outward into all facets of life, in the familial, communal, economic, and political spheres, allowing us to open to *shalom* to the greatest extent possible.

Though much of the emphasis in this book has been on the practice of Centering Prayer, this is just one of many available spiritual practices that Christian contemplatives, mystics, and monastics have drawn on over the centuries. I've included descriptions of several of them below, though this list is by no means exhaustive. See what resonates with you. Be open to being called to the practice that is best suited for where you are on your current path.

CENTERING PRAYER

Centering Prayer is a method based on the thirteenth-century English devotional classic *The Cloud of Unknowing*, which lays the inner groundwork for entering into contemplative prayer. The silence we cultivate during this time prepares the faculties to receive and our hearts to be transformed. It is a consent to God's presence and action within, a God who is nearer than our very breath. It is not intended as a replacement for regular prayer practices, but to provide a deepening and expansive context for them.

1. Choose a sacred word as a symbol of your intention to consent to God's presence and action within. The word should be short and not emotionally charged to limit mental distractions. (Examples: God, Lord, Jesus, Father, Mother, Kyrie, Abba, Love, Agape, Peace, Stillness, Mercy.)

2. Sitting comfortably and with eyes closed, settle briefly. This can simply be an upright, relaxed position in a comfortably sized chair. Keep the back straight, let go of all thought, and then gently and silently introduce the sacred word as the symbol of your consent to God's presence and action within

3. As thoughts arise, return ever so gently to the sacred word as a signal to release the thoughts. Thoughts here include emotions, images, memories, sense perceptions—in short, any distraction.

4. At the end of the prayer period, remain in silence for several minutes to transition back to ordinary flow of consciousness. It may help to have a transitional practice, like reciting a psalm, a verse, or Our Father.

The minimum recommended time to practice is twenty minutes twice a day. The purpose of the practice is not radical change during the experience itself, but during the rest of the day. Do not be discouraged in your practice if you swing from pleasant experiences to emotionally charged experiences. Part of the unfolding process is an unloading, identifying and releasing some of the pain we accumulate and store in our unconscious. This practice is a simple means of cultivating a deepening intimacy with the God who is always already present.

LECTIO DIVINA

Lectio Divina—or Divine reading—is a way of reading Scriptures long practiced by monastics. It consists of multiple slow readings of a small section of Scripture. As you do so, instead of analyzing on the mental level of discursive thought, open yourself to the words, rest in the words, partake of the words, opening up your inmost being to the possibility of insight and transformation.

1. The first stage is *Lectio* or reading. Read the word slowly and reflectively, steeping yourself in it. Short sections, a couple of verses at a time, work best for this practice. There are many sources for short daily meditations, whether in the Book of Common Prayer or many online sources, often associated with monastic or contempla-tive orders.

2. The second stage is *Meditatio* or reflection. Simply reflect deeply on the words and images of the text.

3. The third stage is *Oratio* or response. Leave your thinking aside and let your heart speak to God. This response is inspired by your reflection on the Word of God.

4. The fourth stage of Lectio Divina is *Contemplatio* or rest. As much as possible, let go of all thought and rest in the Word, listening at the deepest level of your being. Open yourself to an inner transformation and realignment according to the Divine presence.

These are general guidelines, not a fixed, formal sequence. The natural movement of the practice is toward an inner silence, allowing deep to call out to deep.

The practice can be done individually or as a group, but if as a group, a facilitator would be required to indicate the movement to the next stage, meaning that there may be less fluid back-and-forth between the stages than with individual practice.

THE JESUS PRAYER

Common in the Eastern Orthodox tradition, the Jesus Prayer consists of a simple but powerful prayer: "Lord Jesus Christ, Son of God, have mercy on me, a sinner." Other variations of this include "Lord, make haste to help me. Lord, make speed to save me!"

Much like the practice of Centering Prayer, it is recommended to say the Jesus Prayer for fifteen to twenty minutes in the morning, before noon, or in the evening. This, in a sense, imprints the prayer on the inner person. When stress or difficult situations arise, the practice is there beneath the surface, and it provides an underlying rhythm where we can find inner equilibrium. After longer experience with the Jesus Prayer, practitioners are sometimes led into the practice of stillness or silent prayer.

WELCOMING PRAYER

Based on the eighteenth-century classic *Abandonment to Divine Providence* by Jean-Pierre de Caussade, the

Welcoming Prayer also involves consent, abandonment, surrender, and trust of the transformative presence of God. It acknowledges the reality of current circumstances and invites the awareness of the Divine within that space. This can be especially helpful throughout the day as a way to counteract our habitual reactions to stress and frustration.

In this practice, we gently become aware of our inner state, physical, mental, emotional, and then simply pray the following:

Welcome, welcome, welcome.
I welcome everything that comes to me in this moment
because I know it is for my healing.
I welcome all thoughts, feelings, emotions,
persons, situations and conditions.
I let go of my desire for security.
I let go of my desire for approval.
I let go of my desire for control.
I let go of my desire to change
any situation, condition, person, or myself.
I open to the love and presence of God and the healing
action and grace within.

WALKING MEDITATION

This practice helps us keep our awareness in the present moment. For many people, the act of walking and maintaining fluid motion encourages an attentive sense of the present. Set aside a specific time to walk, roughly twenty minutes, with no technological devices to distract you, and pay attention to the quality of your awareness. Begin by standing still and taking several slow diaphragm breaths. Follow the breath in and out. Then begin walking. As you walk, gently let thoughts go as they bubble up. Keep your awareness focused on the act of walking, how it feels in different areas of your body, the heels, the soles, the legs, the lungs, the arms. Notice colors and sense impressions on the external level. At the same time, stay attentive to the interior space. Try not to get caught up in thoughts, labels, or mental stories. Notice the rhythm of movement. When you become aware of inner tension, recognize it and let it go. You may need to slow your speed as you go in order to be more aware that you are there simply to enjoy the experience of being a body in motion.

EXAMEN

This practice is a staple of Ignatian spirituality and part of the month-long retreats as practiced by St. Ignatius, founder of the Society of Jesus or Jesuit order. The Jesuit practice is to see God in all things. The Examen is a reflective practice that brings awareness of God at work in our life throughout the day.

1. To begin, sit quietly at the end of the day and ask to see your day through the light of God's eyes

2. Give thanks for the gift of this day.

3. Carefully look back at your experiences of the day, reflecting on where God was present in events, people, and experiences.

4. Be sensitive to shortcomings in life or areas that need attention. Hold them in your awareness and be present with them.

5. Ask for wisdom to discern God's presence in the day to come.

Recommended Reading

Dante

Alighieri, Dante. *The Divine Comedy.* Translated by Allen Mandelbaum. New York: Random House, 1995.

Dreher, Rod. *How Dante Can Save Your Life: The Life-Changing Wisdom of History's Greatest Poem.* New York: Regan Arts, 2015.

Hawkins, Peter S. *Dante's Testaments: Essays in Scriptural Imagination.* Stanford, CA: Stanford University Press, 1999.

Mazzotta, Guisseppe. *Reading Dante* (The Open Yale Course Series). New Haven, CT: Yale University Press, 2014.

Shaw, Prue. *Reading Dante: From Here to Eternity*. New York: Liveright, 2014.

Mythical Perspectives

Campbell, Joseph. *The Hero with a Thousand Faces*. Princeton, NJ: Princeton University Press, 2004

Eliade, Mircea, and Willard R. Trask. *The Sacred and the Profane: The Nature of Religion*. New York: Harcourt, Brace & World, 1959.

Frye, Northrop. *Anatomy of Criticism: Four Essays*. Princeton, NJ: Princeton University Press, 1971.

Heyneman, Martha. *The Breathing Cathedral*. Bloomington, IN: iUniverse, 2001.

Thorpe, Doug. *Wisdom Sings the World: Poetry, Creation, and the Way of Dwelling*. New York: Codhill Press, 2010.

Thorpe, Doug. *Rapture of the Deep*. Pasadena, CA: Red Hen Press, 2007.

Creativity

Brussat, Frederic and Mary Ann. *Spiritual Literacy*. New York: Scribner, 1998.

Cameron, Julia. *The Artist's Way: A Spiritual Path to Higher Creativity*. New York: J.P. Tarcher/Putnam, 2002.

Fox, Matthew. *Creativity: Where the Divine and the Human Meet*. New York: Jeremy P. Tarcher/Putnam, 2002.

Goldberg, Natalie. *Writing Down the Bones: Freeing the Writer Within*. Boston: Shambhala, 1986.

L'Engle, Madeleine. *Walking on Water: Reflections on Faith and Art*. New York: North Point Press, 1995.

Pressfield, Steven. *The War of Art: Break Through the Blocks and Win Your Inner Creative Battles*, 2012.

Spirituality

Benner, David G. *Spirituality and the Awakening Self*. Grand Rapids, MI: Brazos, 2012.

Bodian, Stephan. *Wake Up Now*. New York: McGraw-Hill, 2010.

Bourgeault, Cynthia. *The Heart of Centering Prayer*. Boulder, CO: Shambhala, 2016.

De Mello, Anthony. *Awareness*. New York: Image Books, 1992.

De Mello, Anthony. *The Way to Love*. New York: Image Books, 1995.

De Mello, Anthony. *Sadhana: A Way to God*. New York: Image Books, 1984.

Harvey, Andrew. *Son of Man*. New York: Penguin, 1999.

Keating. Thomas. *Invitation to Love*. New York: Bloomsbury, 1994.

Keating, Thomas. *Open Mind, Open Heart*. New York: Bloomsbury, 2006.

Keating, Thomas. *The Mystery of Christ*. New York: Bloomsbury, 1997.

Kopp, Wolfgang. *Free Yourself of Everything*. Translated by Barbara Wittenberg-Hasenauer. North Clarendon, VT: C.E. Tuttle Company, 1994.

Kornfield, Jack. *After the Ecstasy, the Laundry: How the Heart Grows Wise on the Spiritual Path*. New York: Bantam Books, 2000.

Louth, Andrew. *The Origins of the Christian Mystical Tradition*. New York: Oxford University Press, 2007.

McColman, Carl. *The Big Book of Christian Mystics*. Newburyport, MA: Hampton Roads, 2010.

McColman, Carl. *Christian Mystics: 108 Seers, Saints, and Sages*. Newburyport, MA: Hampton Roads, 2016.

McGinn, Bernard. *The Essential Writings of Christian Mysticism*. New York: Random House, 2006.

Merton, Thomas. *New Seeds of Contemplation*. New York: New Directions, 2007.

Pieper, Josef. *Happiness and Contemplation*. South Bend, IN: St. Augustine Press, 1998.

Ram Dass. *The Only Dance There Is*. New York: Anchor Press, 1974.

Rohr, Richard. *The Naked Now: Learning to See as the Mystics See*. New York: Crossroad, 2009.

Rohr, Richard. *Immortal Diamond: The Search for Our True Self*. Hoboken, NJ: Wiley & Sons, 2012.

Singer, Michael A. *The Untethered Soul*. Oakland, CA: New Harbinger Publication, 2007.

Tolle, Eckhart. *A New Earth: Awakening to Your Life's Inner Purpose*. New York: Penguin, 2008.

Tolle, Eckhart. *The Power of Now*. Vancouver, BC: Namaste Publishing, 2004.

Underhill, Evelyn. *Mysticism: A Study in the Nature and Development of Man's Spiritual Consciousness*. New York: New American Library, 1974.

Vaughan-Lee, Llewellyn. *The Paradoxes of Love*. San Francisco, CA: The Golden Sufi Center, 1996.

Wilber, Ken. *Integral Spirituality*. Boulder, CO: Shambhala, 2007.

Personal Playlist

Waypost	Topic	Author's Playlist	My Playlist
ONE: Waking Up	Self-Aware-ness	"Comfortably Numb"— Pink Floyd, Dar Williams, etc.	

Waypost	Topic	Author's Playlist	My Playlist
TWO: The Burning World	Suffering in the World	"Strange Fruit"— Billy Holiday "Keep on Rocking in the Free World"—Neil Young "Sunday Bloody Sunday"—U2 "Ghost of Tom Joad"—Bruce Springsteen	
THREE: The Burning House	Suffering in the Family	"Mother"— John Lennon "Dear Father"— Colin Hay "Sometimes You Can't Make It on Your Own"—U2 "Mercy Street"— Peter Gabriel "Heavenly Father"—Bon Iver	

Waypost	Topic	Author's Playlist	My Playlist
FOUR: The Burning Self	Confronting the Shadow	"Digging in the Dirt"— Peter Gabriel "Moonshiner"— Bob Dylan "State of Love and Trust"— Pearl Jam	
FIVE: Into the Cathedral	Sabbath and Divine Rest	"O Lord, in Thee Is All My Trust"— Jan Garbarek and the Hilliard Ensemble "What a Day"— Greg Laswell	

Waypost	Topic	Author's Playlist	My Playlist
SIX: Into Nature	Nature and Divine Creativity	"Clam, Crab, Cockle, Cowrie"—Joanna Newsom "Olana"—Marc Cohn	
SEVEN: Into the World	Divine Labor	"Work the Black Seam"—Sting "My Home-town"—Bruce Springsteen	

Waypost	Topic	Author's Playlist	My Playlist
EIGHT: Into Empti-ness	Kenosis and Self-Emptying	"With God on Our Side"—Bob Dylan "Washing of the Water"—Peter Gabriel Sense of Wonder—Van Morrison	
NINE: Into Love	Agape-Love	"Pride (In the Name of Love)"—U2 "You've Been Loved"— Joseph Arthur "I Grieve"—Peter Gabriel	

Waypost	Topic	Author's Playlist	My Playlist
TEN: Into Mystery	Divine Union	"Mystic"—Joshua James "Für Hildegard von Bingen"—Devendra Banhart "Enlightenment"—Van Morrison	

<u>Marc Thomas Shaw</u> is an award-winning instructor, speaker, and author focusing on the contemplative path as a means of inner transformation. A graduate of Fuller Theological Seminary and co-founder of Contemplative Light, he has been a Centering Prayer practitioner for over a decade and is a commissioned presenter through Contemplative Outreach. He is a member of Spiritual Directors International, the Tau Community of Interfaith Franciscans, and the Ignatian Spirituality Project. He co-hosts the Contemplative Light podcast and resides with his family in San Diego, California.

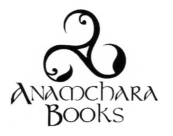

AnamcharaBooks.com

Made in the USA
Middletown, DE
09 March 2019